A LIFE AT WORK

A LIFE AT WORK

The Joy of Discovering
What You Were Born to Do

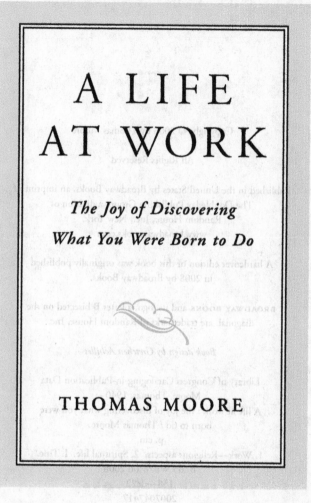

THOMAS MOORE

BROADWAY BOOKS

New York

Published in the United States by Broadway Books, an imprint of
The Doubleday Publishing Group, a division of
Random House, Inc., New York.
www.broadwaybooks.com

A hardcover edition of this book was originally published
in 2008 by Broadway Books.

BROADWAY BOOKS and its logo, a letter B bisected on the
diagonal, are trademarks of Random House, Inc.

Book design by Gretchen Achilles

Library of Congress Cataloging-in-Publication Data
Moore, Thomas, 1940–
A life at work : the joy of discovering what you were
born to do / Thomas Moore.
p. cm.
1. Work—Religious aspects. 2. Spiritual life. I. Title.
BL65.W67M66 2008
158—dc22
2007047417

ISBN 978-0-7679-2253-1

TO BEN MOORE,

A BORN TEACHER, AN EXTRAORDINARY FATHER,

AND A MAGNIFICENT HUMAN BEING

Every person, in the course of his life, must build—starting with the natural territory of his own self—a work, an opus, into which something enters from all the elements of the earth. He makes his own soul throughout all his earthly days; and at the same time he collaborates in another work, in another opus, which infinitely transcends, while at the same time it narrowly determines, the perspectives of his individual achievement: the completing of the world.

Pierre Teilhard de Chardin, *The Divine Milieu*

CONTENTS

CONTENTS

PREFACE

ALCHEMY:
THE OPUS OF THE SOUL

J ust three hundred years ago alchemists like England's John Dee tended a small furnace in their smoky, cluttered laboratory watching closely and patiently for signs of progress. They were seeking medicines, elixirs, and the secret of eternal youth. In their laboratories they had a precious collection of antique books that held the secrets to the process, a tiny oratory with altar and prie-dieu, so they could pray for success, and an oversize record book that served as a log for the experiments they conducted.

For thousands of years, in China and India and later in Europe, men and women alchemists tried to sort out the meaning of life through this exotic system of chemical changes and exotic interpretations. They used a variety of substances—liquids and solids, pure stuff and rotten stuff, ordinary material they found around them and more refined chemicals. They put the material into special vessels, some of them intricate and beautiful glass shapes. They subjected the raw stuff, the *prima materia,* to various levels and periods of heat. All the while they consulted their ancient books and carefully observed changes in color and texture and thought of these changes as images for developments in their hearts and lives.

For some alchemists the goal didn't seem as important as the process. They had special retorts—odd-shaped glass vessels—that would transfer the processed material back into the initial vessel, and they would start all over with their furnaces, books, and notepads, observing further refinements. Some were clearly aiming at a material goal—gold. Others were hoping for a more ethereal and spiritual goal: the making of a self or a soul.

The entire process—not just the finished product—was known as the "opus." The word means "work," and was often capitalized to distinguish it from the more ordinary sense of the word. The "Work" was the long process of refining raw material, going through many phases identified by colors—blackening, whitening, reddening, yellowing—and reaching an end point described variously as a peacock's tail, the philosopher's stone, or the elixir of immortality.

Alchemists used arcane images for the various aspects of the Work, sometimes drawn from religion and mythology, or else their own code. Perhaps they were trying to keep the mysterious Work hidden from those who might profane it—there was often a sense of secrecy about occult practices throughout the centuries. Or maybe they were trying to operate at two levels simultaneously: the mundane and the spiritual. The great mysteries of life are often expressed in rich and sometimes extravagant imagery.

Frequently they distinguished the ordinary sense of things from the spiritual. They spoke of "our" water, "our" sulfur, and "our" mercury, to refer to these things as images rather than literal substances. When you read alchemy you have to remind yourself that black is a mood as well as a literal color. They talked about *aqua per-*

manens, eternal water, to distinguish it from water in its pure physical reality. We might think of alchemical "water" as sheer fluidity, depth, or the flow of life.

The alchemists had to be patient. Some of them never glimpsed their goal, while others labored for years before making any progress. Some had assistants who helped them with all the manual tasks of the work, like John Dee's friend and coworker Edward Kelly. Some had a *soror mystica,* a mystical sister, who helped inspire and sustain the labor.

It has long struck me that these details of the alchemist at work say something profound about anyone's quest to find a life work. It is deep and mysterious. It involves changes and developments. For it, you will need patience, good powers of reflection and observation, and the courage to keep going when it seems nothing of worth is happening. There is a surface activity and an underlying meaning to this work, and to remain on the surface takes you nowhere.

Alchemy offers a model for finding your life work. It teaches that the search is not just about the product but also the process. It offers rich metaphors for the many changes you go through, the moods and emotions you experience, and the repeated failures and successes that are a natural part of the process. Most of all, alchemy takes the search out of the realm of the heroic, where you are desperate to succeed and despair when you fail, into a complex process where the search is a lifelong process.

Still, the alchemist approached his work as though his life depended on it. He believed that the opus is the most important thing you do in life. Your work is equally important, too, not just as a means for making a living but as the medium through which you become a person.

This book is about the search for a life work—not just a job, but an activity or group of activities that gives you a sense of meaning and purpose. It is a book about the spirit and soul of work, and it will provide you with ideas for hearing the call and doing what you were born to do.

A LIFE AT WORK

CHAPTER ONE

GETTING NOWHERE

Pain penetrates me drop by drop.

SAPPHO

I have a friend where I live in New Hampshire who is constantly depressed and frustrated because he can't find the right work. He is one of the most gifted men I know: He's intelligent, has a great sense of humor, loves people and is loved by them, and is an excellent artist. But he can't hold down a job and doesn't know what to do with his life. He hates the torturous rhythm of finding a new career, quitting, and trying again. With a ready smile for the outside world, he's like the classic clown who beneath his happy face paint is desperately sad.

Many men and women are like my friend Scottie. They look relatively happy and get along on the surface of life, but deep down they despair of ever really feeling good about the work they do or believing that their lives have been worth living. They also know too well that unhappiness at work spills over into other areas of life.

The failure to find the right job or to enjoy the one you have creates a special kind of depression. A person may feel that her spirit

has been crushed or perhaps never brought to the light of day. Some wonder why they feel so low and never connect their depression to work. In therapy they may be talking about marital difficulties or an addiction, and they are surprised when their counselor asks about their work. It seems they haven't thought much about work in relation to their emotions and the things that give meaning to their lives.

An opus is the lifelong process of getting life together and becoming a real person, and it is no coincidence that the word is also used for a musical composition or an artist's total production. You are also a work of art—alchemists usually referred to the opus as the Work, but they also called it the Art. You are the artistic designer of your own life, and it is the most important work you will ever do. You will produce things that will make you proud—happy children, a good home, a well-functioning society, and maybe even some decent art. You will become a unique person. Nothing is more beautiful or more valuable. But if that potential goes unrealized, you may despair about life in general.

C. G. Jung once wrote that creativity is an instinct, not an optional gift granted to a lucky few. If you don't find a way to be creative in life, that instinct goes repressed and frustrated. You feel its loss as a deflation, the spirit leaking out of your sense of self. You feel empty, disengaged, and unfulfilled.

The opus doesn't come into existence fully formed. It takes sweat and tears to go through the arduous process of finding yourself, establishing a good career, and making a life. It is especially difficult to achieve all this in a world that doesn't support such a deep, long-term process. Most people don't think beyond the immediate need for money and a bearable job, and most companies don't worry much about the personal calling of their workers.

Today we may not fully appreciate the workplace as a laboratory where matters of soul are worked out. We tend to focus on literal concerns such as pay, product, and advancement, whereas developments in your work life deeply affect your sense of meaning. Doing what you love and having relationships at work that help you as a person can give you feelings of peace and satisfaction at home and in the family.

A recent study of how Americans feel about their work lives concluded that today people are generally happier with their jobs than they were thirty years ago, but they see their work as having a negative impact on life at home. Specifically, they are working longer hours and therefore have less time for their families, their health, and their hobbies. Modern technologies, such as e-mail, blur the borders between work and home. Companies are also offering less in benefits and encouraging employees to work harder for profit sharing and stock ownership. The link between fulfillment at work and happiness at home is more important than ever.

My friend Scottie is a case in point. When I first got to know him, I saw a vibrant man full of talent. I envied him then and still do whenever I see him relaxed and congenial or showing our circle of friends his latest canvas. His talent and personality are extraordinary. I heard about his difficulties with work but thought that all he needed was to search around and find a business that recognized what an asset he would be to them. Naively I wrote a letter of reference for him, thinking that I might solve his problem at one stroke. At that time I looked at the surface of his life; today I'd look deeper.

As time passed, I learned that he had other serious problems, that his family life, so serene on the outside, was apparently troubled and always on the edge of collapse. I was surprised to hear that he had trouble with alcohol dependency and that his occasional outbursts of rage made him feared at home and threatened his marriage. In social settings people are drawn to him like a magnet, but his private life is tragic.

Scottie is having serious trouble finding the right job, staying with the job he has been able to secure, and finding pleasure and fulfillment in what he does. And I mean serious trouble. He stands a good chance of losing an extraordinary partner in his gifted wife and three unusually creative and promising children.

Whatever the source of his problems may be, Scottie's troubled soul is focused now on his inability to find his life work. He secures jobs that offer money and some satisfaction, but he still feels that he is in the wrong place. He gets so frustrated and angry that he distances himself from his family and his friends. He doesn't let anyone help him, and he can't seem to get to the root of his problem.

Scottie is like many people who try to solve the problem of work at a purely practical level: getting new training, trying new careers, and judging success by the size of the paycheck. In fact, the process of finding a job, doing the work, and dealing with the relationships at the workplace has deep roots in family, personal experience, and personality issues. To get to the bottom of serious frustration, you have to consider the whole picture: the past, as well as the present; your family's worldview and experience with work; and the personal issues you bring to the job.

In the ordinary job hunt you may be doing career testing and interviewing and experimenting with jobs, but to move toward your life work you have to work through the past, deep and raw emotions, and relationships that need attention. The roots of career problems run deep, and only a deep solution is effective in the long run.

If you have anything in common with Scottie, I would recommend stopping to look closely at the whole of your life. You will find in this book a long list of things to consider in the inventory of your life experience. Think of every aspect of your life as connected, and always go deeper than you think you need to go.

Stalled: The Feeling of Getting Nowhere

Frustration with work can take many forms. One complaint I frequently hear is the feeling of getting nowhere. Rose, the mother of one of my daughter's friends, has had an excellent education and comes across as an able and creative person. She has ability, intelligence, and a bright personality but still can't move ahead with her career. She tries one job after another, but they seem to be lateral moves. She isn't moving closer to where she wants to be. She feels stalled, stuck, and sometimes even as if she's moving backward.

These days one often hears a plea, expressed with humor or sadness, from men and women, old and young: "What am I going to do with my life?" or "What am I going to be when I grow up?" People in their fifties and sixties say this, meaning that they still don't know for sure who they are and what they are called to do. I have heard Rose say, "I don't know what I'm supposed to do with my life. All I know is that this isn't it."

"What am I going to be when I grow up?" It's a telling remark, suggesting strongly that the person feels that she is still at the beginning of her life, perhaps even a child, immature, not having progressed as far as she should have. The laughter that accompanies the confession covers over concern and anxiety about the situation. "Will I ever grow up? Will I ever succeed?"

If I had such a person in therapy, I'd want to explore the background of this important self-image. Does it play a role in other parts of life? Does it have roots in the family and in early experience? Dealing with the issue outside of the specific work situation might help resolve both the deep emotional problem and the search for a life work.

My friend Scottie has apparently built up a pile of rage as well as depression over the years, knowing that he is capable of doing great things but never able to get a project off the ground. This gap between ambition and achievement can be painful to behold. He is getting nowhere, not by sitting around doing nothing, but by trying again and again without lasting success to do something valuable and worthwhile.

Scottie is angry at himself for being a failure, but he directs his rage against his family. They are close at hand and will keep his secrets—his alcoholism, his anger, and his failures. "Disgruntled" workers notoriously aim their aggression at the people around them; the same is true in a more subtle way in families. The frustration of not having life in gear and not doing the right job transmutes into judgment and rage and, finally, aggression. The feeling of getting nowhere is serious business.

Many people believe that you should always be getting somewhere, that you should always be on the "up" escalator, moving forward in life. But many are not moving anywhere, especially not up. They may feel stuck in a job that feels inferior to them, far beneath their standards and expectations. They may never have found a position even close to their dreams and hopes. Their friends may worry, seeing a person doing work far from his abilities and vision.

People at the top of the ladder can also feel stalled. They have had all the success they dreamed about, and still they feel unfulfilled. I have met many people like this: to all appearances wealthy and successful. They should be happy, but they're not. In many cases it's fairly clear that material rewards simply have not given these "lucky" people the deep satisfaction they crave. Late in the game they may discover that they chose the wrong path or refused an opportunity that would have given them less money but more happiness.

Sometimes people get so discouraged by their failure to find adequate work that they turn against themselves and go looking for a job that has no challenge for them, pays them little, and offers no future. They punish themselves for not succeeding by ensuring that they won't succeed. At one point in his flailing around, Scottie did this: He took a starting position in an automobile dealership though he had no interest in it or talent for the work.

It's clear to me now that Scottie's failure at work has deep roots, perhaps in his past, certainly in his emotions and relationships. When problems with work tie in with other emotional issues like marriage, family, and mood swings, it's clear that the only way to deal effectively with work is to face what Zorba the Greek called "the whole catastrophe."

Dealing with the World

Our own disillusionment isn't the only source of pain and depression with regard to work. The world is out there judging us, expecting things of us, demanding that we do things in their way and not ours. Frustration with work often comes from outside as well as inside.

People get moralistic about work. They tell you that you should make good money, use your talents, get more education, have objectives and goals, and stick to a plan. By these standards, most creative people throughout history appear misguided. They have lived their lives by serendipity, inspiration, and experiment.

You may believe that you have tried too many different things or that you're too old to find a real life work or that you don't have the talent or the calling to do anything significant. People may have judged you so harshly that you lost confidence in yourself. In your pain, you may have turned to alcohol, drugs, or some other numbing distraction, and those addictions in turn cause you to fail at your work.

It takes a well-grounded ego to withstand the assaults of well-intentioned and not-so-well-intentioned critics. But people who are unsure of themselves at work by definition don't have a strong ego. They are vulnerable to attack. They fall over easily when pushed. People in power may have gone through similar trials and now unconsciously force their underlings to remain equally unhappy.

To deal with such pressures, you have to be loyal to your essence or to the person you know you can be. People around you look for evidence of success, but you may have to trust the qualities in you that you know have not yet been revealed. Otherwise you may collapse and have your spirit crushed by criticism and expectations that are not your own.

Many creative people who have contributed much to the human race were not instant leaders and achievers. It took time for them to ripen into the outstanding figures we know them to be. An unexpected source of insight into this matter is the rock musician Sting. He is not only a fine musician but an excellent writer as well, as demonstrated in his penetrating and beautifully honest autobiography, *Broken Music*. There he tells of his early days trying to support himself and find his way. He worked outdoors on building sites as a laborer and then as a bus conductor and eventually as a civil servant. Later, he became a teacher in an elementary school. It was from there that he took a risk and became a professional musician.

Just try to imagine Sting taking your ticket on a bus. What if he stamped your fare and said to you, "I don't know what to do with my life. I don't want to be doing this job when I'm an old man." Knowing where Sting ended up, with wealth and fame, the question is quite a tease. How did he get from one place to the other? Remember, he didn't know that he was going to become Sting. He might have spent the rest of his life as a bus conductor, which might not have been a disaster, but he wouldn't have found an outlet for his unbounded creativity.

His writing describes how pathetic his life was at that time. He had to fill out a form to be a civil servant, and when he was asked about hobbies, all he could write was "walking." He was asked which newspapers he read, and he tried to remember noticing the names of newspapers on the newsstands he saw from the bus, and put those down. He says, "I reckon I would have gotten the job if all they'd done was put a mirror in front of my mouth and checked it for condensation—that's how challenging the interview was."

The scene Sting paints is empty of challenge and vitality, and it is a scene you can find throughout modern life. People compete for jobs that aren't worth the competition. They want to be inspired and challenged in work but often find that they're only called to put in time, to show up and check out.

I'm not saying that ordinary, low-paying jobs can't be inspiring. The point is not the prestige of the work but the attitude of those managing it and doing it. Sting's image is a potent one: putting a mirror in front of his mouth to see if he was alive. There is a zombie quality to many a workplace, and that "living dead" atmosphere betokens a loss of soul. Many people are suffering from the soullessness of their work.

Many times I've heard a man or woman say about their work, "A robot could do it." They feel like "a cog in a machine" or part of a large and cold corporation. They don't see how their effort matters. They see a large portion of their time given over to someone else's profits or to products that don't matter much in the long run.

But even in the darkest situations the human spirit flutters, sings, and sometimes soars. Something in us keeps us focused on a brighter day and a better situation. Those feelings and thoughts of ultimate liberation and success are very important. You can keep them alive, foster them, and gradually turn them into reality. Loyalty to your dreams sometimes appears naive to others, but story after story of successful people indicates that faith in their abilities sustained them and eventually led them to a place of fulfillment.

Especially in times of despair over finding the right work, it would be helpful to read biographies of people who have found their way toward fulfilling work. You will learn how low a person can get and how impossible their prospects may appear, and still, with faith in their abilities, they eventually succeed. They bring with them the values they discovered in times of failure and stagnancy and do their work with added depth.

Sting is a good example. As a successful musician, he sings honestly of human passions and emotions. As a former teacher, he brings weight in language and ideas to his lyrics. As someone who rose up from the depths, he wears his success with a rare maturity. Late in his career, he took a risk and recorded the classical songs of the English composer John Dowland, who is famous for his music about depression and loss.

The point is not merely to succeed but to become a deeper, more complex, more mature person through your struggle. You allow the alchemy of your challenging journey to etch itself into your character, making you into a rich personality. Then whatever work you do will have the quality of your experience and your capacity to be ripened by it.

Doing work that has no soul is the great hidden malady of our time. Clearly, it would be worth our while as individuals and as a society to address unhappiness at work and discover the deep roots of our discontent. The ancient art of alchemy shows a way: Pay attention to your deep and complex interior life, become more sensitive about your relationships, consider your past thoughtfully, and use your imagination at its full power. Work from the ground up toward finding the work that will make your life worthwhile.

The following chapters offer ways of bringing your soul to life so that you can see a possible future. They contain strategies for engaging your depths and your vision, going deep and going high, to bring your whole self into the process. Only when you are fully engaged can you see the activity that will make your life feel worth living.

CHAPTER TWO

THE CALLING

The Lord whose oracle is in Delphi neither indicates
clearly nor conceals but gives a sign.

HERACLITUS

Mahud was a simple man who lived in a small village and made his living by selling vegetables at a busy market. He was comfortable enough and liked his work. But one day the angel Khabir appeared to him and told him to jump in the river. Without thinking about it, Mahud leaped into the flowing water.

He was carried downstream until a man on shore threw him a rope and pulled him out. The man offered Mahud a job in his fishing business and a small room where he could live. Mahud appreciated the man's kindness and took the job and worked at it, rather happily, for three years. Then Khabir appeared to him once more and told him to move on.

Mahud obeyed immediately and walked from village to village until in one place a man offered him a job in his fabric shop. This was new to Mahud, but he took the job and learned the trade and worked there relatively happily until the angel appeared again and sent him on. Mahud worked at odd jobs for years in this manner, always moving along when the angel instructed.

When Mahud was an old man, he had gained the reputation of a holy man. People began coming to him with their illnesses and worries begging him for cure and counsel. One day a visitor to his village asked him, "Mahud, how did you get to where you are now?"

Mahud thought for a moment and said, "It's difficult to say."

It's difficult to say because Mahud's only talent was his openness to the directives coming from the angel whose name means "The All Aware." Mahud had the precious ability to recognize the call to move on and the openness of heart to follow it.

This is a story about calling and obedience to the call. But let's remember that at root *obedience* means "listening." To find your way you have to pay close attention to the signs about when to change your job, when to get unstuck and reenter the flow of life, and when to retire to a life of healing and teaching.

Unfortunately for us, perhaps, an angel isn't going to physically appear and tell us what to do next. But the angel of the story does represent something that is real for all of us: a sense of destiny, vocation, and direction. The word *vocation* comes from the Latin word *vox*, voice. A vocation is a call.

Why would a sense of direction in life be called a "vocation"? Is the voice of the angel only supernatural or mystical? Or is there something natural about the capacity of life to "speak" to us and give us hints about where to go?

The question is not so much does the world give us a direction, but are we able to read the world for its information? We tend to look at the surface of events and deal with them practically. An alternative is to see events as symbols, images, and signs.

Let me offer an example from a key turning point in my life. I had been a Catholic seminarian as well as a brother in a religious order for thirteen years. I had studied spirituality, theology, philosophy, and the Bible. I was thoroughly prepared for the priesthood. But when I went to an ordinary parish church for the first time and gave a sermon, not as a priest but as a priest-to-be, I was shocked at the gap between my contemporary studies and ideas and the much more traditional views of the people I was speaking to. I was shaken by that experience and took it as a sign to reconsider my vocation. Was I called to fight the battle of liberal theology versus the church authorities and a conservative community? Or should I move on to something else? I read the signs carefully and with great intellectual and emotional difficulty decided to try something new.

The concrete, visible, material world speaks to us, if we would only listen. You don't have to do exactly what the signs indicate, but it would help to consider them in evaluating the status of your work life. For example, if you are failing in a particular line of work, your difficulty may not mean that you are lacking or at fault, but that you are in the wrong profession.

You also have to attend to your interior life to a degree that you can also sense your calling from internal indications. It may be a strong interest, a feeling of magnetism, pleasure, or joy around a particular kind of work, or blissful daydreams. On the other hand, distaste and discomfort on a job may also be a sign to move on. Difficulty at work can stem from many different sources, one of them the mere fact that you are unsuited for the job. Or it may mean that you have lessons to learn and need to stay and be present for them. You have to read your dissatisfaction and your problems at work to find their meaning and take them as signs. One of the goals of this book is to show how you can attend to and interpret these signs.

I had a colleague once who, while teaching at a university, was denied tenure and fought it with every resource he could conjure up. He and I had very different temperaments, and perhaps it was only natural that he would fight, in that situation, while, when my turn came up, I read being denied tenure as a sign again to move on. Still, I think he would have been a happier person if he had been more flexible generally and willing to listen to the guidance of life around him. I had the feeling that he simply couldn't imagine himself in another line of work, and he stayed, even though all signs pointed him in a different direction.

The signs that tell you to make a move, stay where you are, or change something about your situation come in many forms. It may be trouble at work, as in the case of my colleague at the university. It could be a strong desire to be in another occupation. Maybe you spend more time and energy at an activity outside of your work, indicating that you could find a way to make that activity your job.

I know a man who was quite successful in running businesses, but he spent more time in programs for children at a nearby park than he did at work. Eventually he saw what was happening, quit his job, and became a full-time teacher in a school athletic program. He is happy with his work and has no regrets about making less money.

Sometimes the signs are more difficult to read. You may get headaches, stomach upsets, or frequent colds that interfere with the work you're doing. Obviously, physical symptoms such as these may have nothing to do with work, but sometimes they may reflect tension and stress that come from being in the wrong job or not doing it in a way that satisfies.

Tensions in the marriage or family may also be related to dis-

satisfaction at work, yet people often don't read these signs in relation to the job. They assume that all family tensions have to do with
family interactions, whereas unhappiness at work can function as a
root emotional problem radiating into other apparently unrelated
parts of life.

Psychoanalysis has taught us to read the events of daily life and
our ordinary emotions with considerable subtlety and imagination.
The most ordinary action or object can be a symbol for something
truly significant and deep-rooted.

If you are making mistakes at work, you might well be sab-
otaging yourself or your employer. Your anger and aggression may
be coming out so indirectly that you don't recognize what you
are doing. If you could read these mistakes as signs, you might be
able to trace your anger and discover what is really bothering
you. Then you can make a more intelligent decision about your
career.

If you can read the signs in your work, you can adjust and perhaps avoid unnecessary failures. In my work in television and video
production, I have met many creative people, but none as impres-
sive as Robert, who, as far as I know, has never had a full-time job.
He makes documentary films and he produces very imaginative
large public programs. He told me that he is very good at coming
up with fresh ideas and putting on a successful show. But whenever
he tries to repeat a program and make a series out of it, he fails. So
he has found a way to be a "starter." He produces only first-time
events and then turns his successful idea over to someone else to
keep the project going.

This may not sound like a brilliant solution, but I can imagine
many people believing that they should carry their projects
through, even though they know they will fail. Robert has the

imagination and emotional freedom to let go of the part of a project he knows he can't do. He has read the signs and adjusted.

Called by Whom? By What?

A calling is the sense that you are on this earth for a reason, that you have a destiny, no matter how great or small. Those who look at life more soberly might question whether such an attitude is warranted. It may seem naive. But the sense of calling doesn't necessarily require belief in the supernatural and it doesn't have to be naive.

A calling is a sensation or intuition that life wants something from you. It can give meaning to the smallest acts and helps create a strong identity. If you have a reason for being, you don't feel entirely aimless. You know who you are and what to do. In a culture where existential anxiety—the worry that nothing is of value and nothing makes sense—is still the order of the day, these are valuable realizations.

Those who believe in God or a higher power or in the intelligence of nature and life have little trouble recognizing the legitimacy of a sense of calling, but still they might feel it lacking in their own lives. Their problem may be that they put too much wishfulness into their belief, expecting life to serve them their destiny in clear and concrete terms. They may want specific direction without the quest and search and sorting out that is also part of the human condition.

In the 1980s I gave frequent workshops and lectures at the Dallas Institute of Humanities and Culture. It was an exciting venture, working with James Hillman, Patricia Berry, Gail Thomas, Robert Sardello, and others developing "archetypal psychology" and exploring the soul of culture. A woman full of ambition and energy came to several of my workshops, and one day she told me she felt a strong calling to do the exciting work she saw teachers at the institute doing.

I was concerned right away because she didn't have the educational background to join the rest of us, who had many years of study behind us. But she tried. She gave a workshop and then a lecture. Of course they didn't go well and were an embarrassment to her and the institute. So she went back to the city she came from and tried to do the same thing there. Again, she failed. She was a dance instructor, and finally she got the idea of teaching dance in a special way informed by the ideas she had picked up at the institute. She was very effective at this work, and for many years afterward she fulfilled her calling.

The initial revelation of a life work may be highly emotional but unformed. A person may believe she is called to be just like someone she admires, but then she has to learn how to adapt that calling to her own abilities and temperament. It may take time for the calling to be fully revealed, if it ever is. It may also entail fumbling for a period of time, making mistakes, and failing.

As you will discover in the chapters ahead, chaos and calling go together. In your confusion and experimenting, you learn about the laws of life and you feel the burden of your existence. This is not a bad thing because it gives weight to your thoughts and gives character to your work. If you only toss around in chaos or latch onto a source of meaning without self-questioning and wonder, your convictions will lack the weight and bite of real life.

I never hear my friend Scottie talk about a calling or a need to serve or the desire to really do something with his life. He seems concerned about the details of whatever job he has at the moment. He never talks about his vision, except to say that he doesn't know what to do with his life. Maybe he needs to step back, think about things, have a big conversation about life in general, and eventually find his calling.

Monks are forever talking about their vocation. They don't talk about talents or wishes; they speak of being called. Work that requires complete dedication, like that of the monk, is so vast in scope that a mere aptitude isn't sufficient to explain a person's choice of profession. That could be true of a doctor or politician who feels called to be of service to humankind.

The story of Mahud suggests that any kind of job is a calling, no matter how ordinary. Maybe we elevate certain work, like that of doctors and politicians, and refer to it as a calling, overlooking the vocation to whatever work is our destiny. Most of us live within relatively narrow perimeters and enjoy a small life. There is beauty and satisfaction in that smallness, partly because the least significant of lives can still have cosmic proportions for the meaning and purpose they offer.

A person who shows special skill at a small craft, such as making wooden bowls or simple jewelry, is engaged in universal values of beauty and expressiveness. A bookkeeper or an accountant plays a role in the financial vitality of a community and even a nation. Honesty and care are as important in small things as they are in big things.

Samuel Beckett once wrote a quirky novel called *Mercier and Camier* about two men taking a walk around the block. Beckett tells the story as though these two were Dante and Virgil canvassing the whole of creation. He uses mythic language and large concepts to the point of comic absurdity. But our lives are like that: As we go about our small lives, constantly bumping into the great issues of love and death, meaning and ignorance, we, too, are comic. A sense of destiny can keep us in touch with that larger picture and gives profound significance to the insignificant things we do.

It's tempting to inflate the notion of calling, to imagine it as a great revelation on a mountaintop, a once-and-for-all pronouncement of who we are and what we are to do. But Mahud has several "callings," which together lead him to an unexpected ultimate life work: healing, counseling, and holiness.

At the end, Mahud's openness to his many callings leads him to develop into a character of extraordinary depth and power, so much so that people come to him for help. He has gathered together no coherent set of skills from his work that would explain his effectiveness as a healer. Only his openness to destiny has given him his ultimate life work, and at that point it's clear that the work he has done has been not just simple labor but internal development of character. The two are inseparable: the work that we do and the opus of the soul.

The Willingness to Change

People's idea of a career can become monolithic. You spend years of education and apprenticeship to acquire the skills of a job, and you feel that investment as a heavy weight. You identify with your work, and the idea of changing it entails a personal reversal. If you change jobs, you change "who you are."

The financial security developed over the years in a particular position may give you some flexibility to search out alternatives, but at the same time it may prevent you from detaching yourself from that career and starting over somewhere else. For many people security is a heavy weight around them that won't let them consider a serious change in direction.

The idea of a calling can also be monolithic. You are called to be a doctor, and so you can't imagine doing anything else. Or you are called to be a musician but you work for the post office and play in a band on weekends. You can't picture yourself as a full-time musician because in your mind it isn't who you are.

Thus the benefit of thinking of a multiplicity of callings rather than a single call to a profession. You may be called to be many things at once or one thing after another. You may be called to be a parent and a librarian, a husband and a mechanic, a fund-raiser and an artist. You may be called to be a nurse for a portion of your life and then discover a new calling to be a professional calligrapher. Many people have found their life work by making unexpected shifts in the work they do.

For some people the various callings penetrate one another and come together. I feel this about myself. I have been a monk, a teacher, a musician, a therapist, and a writer. I have been surprised how as a writer about the soul, I have been invited to speak in pulpits of many different religions and denominations. As I ascend the steps to the high perch of the pulpit, I often remember how as a teenager I wanted so desperately to be a priest speaking about the soul. Now here I am, a married person, making a living writing books, but still somehow fulfilling my dream of being a priest.

My work has led me into a friendship with the actor Martin Sheen. I remember watching him in films when he was a young man and being astonished at his talent. But he is also a social activist who supports a variety of causes and has been jailed for his actions. Now, is he called to be an actor, an activist, or both?

It seems important to nurture a strong sense of calling while not fixing on any particular form of work. This capacity to be flexible may be one of the most significant strengths in relation to a life work because it allows movement. Life is not usually monolithic, narrowly focused, or unchanging. Just the opposite; life is a flowing, shifting force that rushes over obstacles and seems bent on movement and transitions. If we don't adjust to this torrent of vitality, we may have to become rigid in order to hold on to a job or career, and that rigidity causes many emotional problems.

When I was young I was sometimes criticized strongly for pursuing my many interests and for entering and then quitting careers. Then when I became an author, interviewers would look at that same life and say, "How interesting. Tell us about it. How did you do it?"

If flexibility is the primary virtue as you pursue your callings, then a philosophy of the polycentric life—the idea that you can be more than one thing—is a close second. This important lesson I learned in my early association with the psychologist James Hillman, who turns many common assumptions upside down to reveal the straitjackets we have willingly put on for years. In his view, a monocentric view in anything is bound to create rigidity and moralism.

Those who criticized me for going after too many dreams were speaking from a one-eyed place. They could only see one goal at a time, and they got judgmental whenever they suspected any deviation from that standard. I have applied Hillman's principle of polycentricity as a therapist in many situations and have found it to be a philosopher's stone, a discovery that becomes the source of insights and solutions. It works magic, just when the situation appears hopeless.

A woman tells me, "I'm a nurse. I'm interested in psychology. I want to be an artist. I'm fragmented. I can't get my life together." In that worry, instead of "fragmented," a word of judgment, I hear "multitalented." Instead of trying to get her life together, I think, "How can she do all of it comfortably?"

Many people believe that they should be *whole*, meaning that their life and work should look like one piece. They have never questioned this word *whole,* or imagined it in a way that doesn't pressure them to give their life a single focus. An alternative would be to appreciate a multifaceted work life, to give attention to the many interests that claim your attention.

Often this pressure appears as a dilemma: "Should I quit my job as a nurse and become a psychologist? Which way should I go?" Maybe you should go both ways—and more. You will need a rich, flexible imagination guiding you toward a solution where you are not torn apart, where you at least give some of your energy to your various interests. People will judge you, of course, because the dominant value in society is unity and single-mindedness. But you don't have to think that way. You can operate out of a personal philosophy of polycentricity—many centers of interest and attention.

"I want to be an artist but I love my work as head of a thriving business," a man says. "Isn't there some way to do both?" Remember Wallace Stevens, one of America's greatest poets? He was an insurance executive and seemed to thrive at his job even as he wrote complex, brilliant poems. About his motive for becoming an insurance executive, he was quite clear: "I didn't like the idea of being bedeviled all the time about money and I didn't for a moment like the idea of poverty, so I went to work like anybody else and kept at it for a good many years."[1] He consistently appreciated ordinary labor, and yet he wrote to his wife that poetry is really what made his life worthwhile.[2]

Barbara, a woman I have known for many years, who has never found her life work, says she wants to do family therapy, though she is very aware of her talent as an illustrator. Meanwhile, she suspects there is yet another calling waiting to be heard. She doesn't know now what that might be. At this point at least, she might pursue many possibilities at once—take a class in psychology while working freelance as an illustrator, for example.

A calling is a deep sense that your very being is implicated in what you do. You feel that you fit into the scheme of things when you do this particular work. You have a sense of purpose and completion in the work. It defines you and gives you an essential tranquillity.

The work that provides such a deep reward may change over time, and you may go through several periods in your life defined by a different work. Toward the end of your life you may see all the jobs you have done as fateful, composing your life work and answering your calling.

I once counseled a priest in his seventies who didn't feel that he had a calling to the priesthood, even though he had spent over fifty years as a priest. He regretted giving his life to something he didn't feel called to do, and he felt bitter and depressed in his old age. He would bring me paintings of his dreams, and we would sit there staring at the striking, colorful images on the floor between us, and we would look for a way out of the bitter regret. I had met him in a course I was teaching for art therapists, and he was discovering mild joy in self-expression and psychology. Though bitter to him, his regret and depression didn't repel people; on the contrary, people were drawn to him and loved him. I had the impression that although he came late to the realization that he didn't fully want the role he had lived all his life, he had done good work and was now following a new calling that gave him real satisfaction. He constantly talked about his depression, but at the same time he was finding new vitality.

I think this man did indeed have a calling to the priesthood, which he carried out very well. But he came to a point where he tasted the world he had given up for his vows and he badly wanted this new life. It was a sad situation, but it was bittersweet, because his sadness only made him more human and more connected to the people around him. His joy and sense of humor were muffled by the depression, but they were present. Here was a man on the cusp between two callings, one colored by regret and the other seemingly impossible for his age. At least, that is the way he felt. Eventually, his optimism came to the foreground, and without losing the depressive current in him, he was able to be what for him was a new kind of priest, now skilled in counseling and art therapy and more aware of the struggles people go through.

Loyalty to Your Calling

A strong call to a career or particular work is a precious thing. It gives a shape to your entire life and helps your relationships by quelling the search for an identity that is always implicated in the quest for a life work. But once you perceive your calling, you may still have problems because, as with this priest, circumstances might well work against it.

People feel called to work for which they have no background or education. It may take a great effort to get that education late in life or after having gone in a different direction previously. When I was a college professor I counseled many women returning to school after years of raising a family. It was difficult for these women to shift their orientation from home to school, and I was always impressed with the courage and loyalty most of them brought to the work they felt compelled to do. In some cases their husbands or children didn't agree with their choice, and they had to move ahead toward their calling without the support they wanted. Many felt embarrassed being in classes with young men and women their children's age. And yet, with their eyes focused on their goal of a life work, they persevered.

They didn't see college as a complete break with their job of raising their children. Their calling involved both elements: family and a job. But they had to make the transition, and that was the most difficult task. One woman I remember in particular, Patsy, had always engaged in fund-raising for community causes while she was raising her family, and when the children left home and she got her degree in school, she became more focused and professional about her work. Her ability to help nonprofit organizations raise money now became a profession rather than a pastime. She set up an office, hired some help, and attracted clients. Her transition was not toward a new direction in life but toward a more formal and ultimately more satisfying leadership role as a professional.

We live in a pragmatic age when people often value the predictable standards of success. They may steer their friends toward practical goals. In this environment, you have to keep your sights on the vocation you feel within you, though it is not always easy to champion the interior life when the external world is pressing in.

There is something almost simpleminded about Mahud's willingness to do whatever the angel says. He simply jumps into the river, an ancient image for the ongoing flow of life. He is willing without any hesitation to be part of life. That commitment to vitality is allied to the commitment to a calling. Both take you to a place you may never have known, but once there, you know it is what you have been looking for all the while.

CHAPTER THREE

SOUL AND SPIRIT

Life seems glorious for a while, then it seems poisonous. But you must never lose faith in it, it is glorious after all. Only you must find the glory for yourself. Do not look for it either, except in yourself; in the secret places of your spirit and in all your hidden senses.

WALLACE STEVENS

Many years ago I discovered the seminal work of a priest, theologian, musician, and therapist of fifteenth-century Italy, Marsilio Ficino. He inspired artists, educators, and even politicians toward making a world focused on values of friendship, beauty, and spirituality. He was a magus, someone who enjoyed special powers of healing and teaching that were not due to mere training or abstract knowledge. His mother was a psychic, and apparently he inherited deep and effective powers of intuition. A magus is someone, he said, who is plugged into the powers and mysteries of nature like the branch of an alien tree grafted onto a tree of a different species.

I spent many summers in my youth on our family's farm in upstate New York. Next to the old house was a single tree that bore two kinds of apples and plums, the result of grafting done by my ancestors over a hundred years ago. This is Ficino's image for being a magus, and, I would add, being connected to your soul: grafting yourself to your deep nature so that its fruitful juices flow through you.

In all my work I have tried to revive Ficino's role of magus to bring more humane values to our world. It may take some magic to find the work that heals you and makes you feel alive. If you are not grafted onto your nature and to the source of your life, you may be doing work that is dry and infertile. You don't feel good doing it because it isn't part of the system that includes all three parts: you, nature, and work. It is cut off and doesn't have the juice that soul would give it.

To be grafted to soul means to be open to the life that pools deep inside you, allowing it to coalesce into a career or other kind of work. Your choice of work flows from who you are—from your interests, tastes, hopes, and values. As you work, you feel that you are doing something consonant with your nature. You aren't working against yourself, not contradicting the person you are.

Here is my starting point in looking for a life work: Step out of the frenzied pursuit of the right job, look around at the whole of your life, and connect with the source of your vitality. If you begin with who you are and with the current of life you feel inside you, you will be grounded as you search and experiment. Your quest will be like a spring flowing from the font of your very nature, rather than a mere maddening search for a suitable occupation or position.

Ficino himself led an odd but highly creative life. When he was very young, the wealthy Cosimo di Medici offered Ficino's family a deal. If they educated their son in Latin and Greek and made him a man of letters, Cosimo would give him a villa near Florence where he could act as Cosimo's intellectual adviser and translator.

Ficino's father, who was a physician, agreed to the deal. The son spent his life studying, translating, and gathering people together for discussion and the serious exchange of ideas. He brought music, painting, literature, and architecture into the mix, and eventually he even became a priest.

I doubt that I, or my readers, will ever be offered a villa in Tuscany, but there are some ways in which we could emulate Ficino. We could see our life work less as a typical job and more as the cultivation of beauty, healing, community, and friendship—Ficino wrote often about the importance of friendship. The work you ultimately decide to do may be influenced by your interest in matters of soul, and you may learn that a life work rises up out of a heart and imagination that you have tended and educated over the years. Your vision about the whole of life gives you a basis for choosing what to get involved with.

Ficino described the soul as the central unifying factor that needs to be alive in both people and society. But we have a rather soulless work culture dedicated to machinelike productivity and ego rewards of success, money, prestige, and advancement. It may seem impractical to take a lesson from Ficino and make a soulful life the primary goal. But you can cultivate the soul in your own life and in society, and at the same time find exciting work to do. This chapter will show you what work looks like when you begin with who you are, soul and spirit.

Breathing with Your Soul

The soul is what makes you a unique person, a human being with deep feelings and the capacity for strong relationships. Your soul comes alive in cherished friendships, family gatherings, and the care you bring to your home. And yet, it isn't easy to define or even describe with any clarity. It's the mystery element in your sense of who you are and in the world you engage with.

Writing about the soul, the Greek philosopher Heracleitus emphasized depth: "You could never find the limits of the soul, no matter how many roads you took, so deep is its mystery." *Deep* is perhaps the best word to describe the experience of the soul—deep feelings, deep thoughts, deep connections, deep projects. Soul is there in the most ordinary circumstances of life, but it is their mystery and their depth.

Tradition connects the soul to the breath, both literal and metaphorical. You have a soul if you are breathing and show some signs of life. But you also need to breathe in a less literal way, taking life in and breathing it out: winning and losing, being happy and being sad, beginning a project and ending it, entering relationships and leaving them. This is the bittersweet rhythm of an engaged life, and it is a sign that you have a soul.

Sometimes people get stuck, and the rhythm stops. They can't take in new possibilities or they can't let go of old and tired patterns. Psychology talks about being fixated, frozen in a relationship or a view of yourself or a troublesome habit. Soul gets lost when life can't go on its rhythmic way, and soullessness is the ultimate cause of deep dissatisfaction.

Everyone is frozen somewhere in their lives. I know a couple who have two talented, well-behaved children, but they understand parenthood essentially as exercising harsh authority. That is how they both grew up and the only way they can act. Their children are unhappy and occasionally react against their parents by failing at school. They seem to fail consciously to disappoint their parents.

In conversation with the parents it was immediately apparent that they can't exit the tight view of parenthood they have always known. They are only imitating their own strict parents and are frozen in a fantasy, stuck in a philosophy that is completely unconscious and yet creating havoc in their household. They want to explore new possibilities, but their inherited pattern lies so deep, they aren't even aware of how much it affects them.

These parents could give their children some air, create an atmosphere in which they could breathe: succeed and fail, experiment and learn important values, play hard and work hard. As it is, you don't see these signs of the breath in the way they are raising their children. The atmosphere in their home is stifling and anxious. No one can comfortably pursue their dreams of happiness, because they are so focused on what is expected of them.

Loving Your Work

When the soul is alive in us we can make connections, be involved, and feel in touch with the people around us and the things we do. Connectedness is another hallmark of the soul. It's important in our work not only to be excited about being successful and making money, but also deeply concerned about the value of what we're doing and having a stake in the outcome or product. If you can take romanticism and sentimentality out of the word, you could say that it's necessary to *love* what we're doing and what we're making. People who are frustrated with their work often say they simply don't love what they're doing and therefore feel unmotivated to get to work. Love is the impetus that propels us toward our life work.

The ancient Greeks told of a union between Eros, the spirit of love, and Psyche, the soul. When you have a soul, you are capable of loving your work and the things you create. Much of the pain people feel in work is the absence of love, which implies a lack of

soul, as well. The ancient image of Eros and Psyche as a loving couple suggests that to love your work you have to do it with soul, and
to have soul in your work you have to love it in some way.

Loving your work doesn't mean liking every minute or being
passionate about everything you do. Love can be a quiet hum in the
background, a basic feeling that the work you're doing has value,
fits you, and matches a desire to accomplish something.

Some people labor hard at a job and find it difficult, but still
feel deep down that it is the work they want to do. Love can be subtle, steady, and invisible. Yet many people don't have this underlying love. They feel that they're doing the wrong thing. It takes a
great effort for them to get up and go to work because they don't
have any of that deep, motivating, invisible love.

We're back to Sting's mirror with no sign of a living, breathing
person. The job environment he encountered in the civil service
office was soul dead. It didn't inspire any enthusiasm, interest, or
challenge—signs of love, or even the potential for love. If you find
yourself in such a situation, you have several choices: You can wait
for something better, find a place that does have love, or bring your
own love to the place.

You feel your soul present in work when *you* are present, when
you are not just going through the motions or putting in time. But
you can't enjoy that soulful condition if the job doesn't allow for it
or if you are not in a place yourself where soul can appear. The right
job and the right attitude go together to release the soul and give
your work vitality.

Intimacy is another sign of soul. Many of the things we do today we do at a distance. We work in factories at a specific job and
never see the result of our labor. The assembly line can keep soul
out by making the repetitive tasks meaningless in terms of out-

come. You not only have to see the object you have helped make, you have to love it.

This talk of love may seem completely out of place in relation to contemporary work life. It may seem more a luxury than an essential. That is because we tend to think in purely pragmatic terms. We worry about profit, efficiency, and productivity so much that important human issues go unnoticed. Whatever the work, however exalted or menial, a person *needs* the basic human experiences of intimate connection and love.

Without soul, work is bound to be painful. You make great effort, spend valuable time, and at least subliminally look for deep rewards, but the soul stuff is missing. Most people couldn't put a name to what they sense is lacking, because it seems quite mysterious and intangible. C. G. Jung said that loss of soul is a "pathological event and the cause of neurosis."[1] The Portuguese poet Fernando Pessoa wrote a poem called "There are sicknesses worse than sicknesses," in which he describes in strong images the sensations of loss of soul:

> *My soul came apart like an empty jar.*
> *It fell overwhelmingly, down the stairs.*
> *Dropped from the hands of a careless maid.*
> *It fell. Smashed into more pieces than there was china in the jar.*

Without soul, work may feel empty. You have to force yourself to do it and you readily find distractions for relief. In your imagination you may think of many other jobs you could do—you are physically present at the job but mentally and emotionally you're far away. In your frustration you may become angry at your employer, your workmates, or the job itself.

Soul also grants individuality. If you are not a person of soul, you probably think like the crowd and go after the rewards that everyone takes for granted as being desirable. You may think like the culture at large or your region or your family or your church, and you may be quite unconscious of the influence of these groups on you. Part of finding your soul is to wake up to this habit of thinking like others and go your own way. It may be painful to separate from those people who have given you a sense of belonging and purpose, but your soul is at stake.

A few years ago I was asked by the FBI to speak to spiritual counselors who offer therapy to agents from the field. I made the effort to fly from New Hampshire to Seattle to meet with these people because I realized how important their work is.

The participants in the program were people of various ages and religious backgrounds. I found them warm, open-minded, and eager to get a few ideas that might help them. Their sense of humor and friendliness also impressed me. These were people working in the trenches with agents who deal with corruption and the worst kind of criminality.

One of the issues we discussed was the role of religious diversity in an age when various faiths are bumping into one another on an increasingly small planet. Traditional ideas about religion and spirituality are changing rapidly and radically. Toward the end of the discussion, a man stood up and made an emotional statement about his experience of separating from his faith community.

He had been a conservative pastor for a traditional religious church for many years. He preached a fundamentalist approach to Christianity and was the perfect leader for his congregation, which wanted to keep to the old ways. But, he said in a confession that was so deeply felt and honestly expressed that you could just feel hearts going out to him in this counselors' group, the years of attending the FBI sessions had affected him deeply. He had grown in ways that his church community at home would never understand or accept. He had spent intense hours of deep conversation with other counselors who had very different beliefs but impressed him with their sincerity and conviction. He had heard many talks from highly qualified spiritual leaders about accepting diversity of belief. Over the years these conversations and inspirational talks got through to him and his mind and heart opened up.

Personally, he was happy and grateful for the changes—his new openness and his more subtle understanding of his faith—but he said that it was very difficult for him to be himself with these views in his community. He had very old friendships and church relationships that would be threatened if he expressed his more liberal ideas and went in his own direction. Even his wife, he said, would not understand how he had lost his old certainties about belief, morality, and religious identity. His openness would mark him as being different from who he had been and how snugly he fit into his old community.

This man was going home to face the emotional struggle of separation out of his former unconscious state and away from the community that shared the unconsciousness. He wasn't making any judgments about them but only trying to find a way to keep his old life while moving in new directions in his thinking.

In alchemy one of the first important developments in the opus is a process called *separatio*. The alchemist puts a significant amount of stuff into a vessel and watches closely as the elements separate out. This is a crucial stage, for progress in the opus is possible only if separation takes place effectively.

I believe that the pastor in Seattle was deep in the process of *separatio*, in his case the separation of his own thinking and values from the tightly packed thoughts and morals of a community in which he had lived all his life. There was a lot at stake in the process for him. The way he described it, he seemed to feel that he had to choose between his unfolding self and the people who made up his world.

His story is a good example of what it takes to be an individual and have a soul. It requires internal work that may demand unanticipated heroic efforts. Men and women sometimes go through a painful sorting out of their beliefs and values as they discover a deeper and better world. They have to deal with the people around them who haven't gone through that shift in vision.

When I speak of finding soul in your work so that you might discover the joy of labor, I'm not talking about something simple and easy. It may be the most challenging thing of all to crawl out of the pleasant unconsciousness that has been your womb for many years and enter life as a grounded, thoughtful individual.

In this regard, people often see talk about the soul as conservative and unchallenging, while I believe it is a radical challenge to live boldly from the heart and create a different and better society. If you wake up to your soul, you may have to stand apart from the crowd and dare to be unique.

The soul is your depth, like the rich earth nourishing a flower. It is always there, and it has always been there. From it your life emanates and blossoms. You glimpse it in your deepest emotions and the very roots of your thinking. It is hidden in your past and not yet fully visible in your actual life. As it shows itself, you realize how much of an individual you are, even eccentric and sometimes mad.

The Uplifting Spirit

The spirit is quite different from the soul, and it, too, should be in harmony with your life work. Spirit is the upper region of experience and includes your worldview, ethical sensitivities, ideas about life and death, religious beliefs and understandings, and intellectual development. It is growth, adventure, experiment, advance, and discovery.

When I use the word *spirit* in this context, I don't restrict its meaning to "spirituality" in the modern sense. I mean spirit as a portion of who you are and how you live, in broad terms. Unlike the deeply embedded soul, spirit is high, up in the stratosphere of our thinking. If you have a philosophy of life and a set of values, if you have a passionate vision and ambitions, these are largely expressions of your spirit.

It's obvious that a church or temple is a place of spirit, but so, too, is a school, a university, or a corporate headquarters. A book club probably has a lot of spirit in it—people reading various authors and exchanging ideas. It probably has soul as well in its intimacy and ordinariness. Universities tend to flaunt the spirit. They are protective of their campuses—areas marked out from the mundane and ordinary. They speak of "higher" education and others see them as being ivory towers, a good image of the skyward movement of spirit.

Church steeples, skyscrapers, pagodas, and even hotel "towers" are symbolic embodiments of a strong spirited imagination. You find spirit in ambition, forward thinking, futurism, speed, and development. In contrast, soul appreciates the old, the past, memory, and tranquillity.

Spirit and soul are two dynamics moving in different directions: One reaches into the past for inspiration, the other moves steadily into the future. Soul thrives on memories and old attachments, while the spirit wants to move on.

Speaking as a representative of soul, I may unwittingly give the impression that soul is better. Not so. Spirit and soul are both essential and each is best when linked closely to the other or when they overlap so much that it's difficult to sort out one from the other. They influence each other: Your inspiring image of a better world might be rooted in the humble values you learned from your family. Your ambitions for a great career may have their roots in a passing comment from a relative or teacher in your childhood.

Difficulty with work can involve wounds to the spirit, as well as to the soul. You may have strongly felt convictions and expectations about who and what you want to be, and your current job may be so distant from those hopes that you despair of ever having your dreams fulfilled. You feel that your spirit is inhibited or crushed.

You may have important values that the workplace offends. You would like to work for a company, say, that is sensitive to community values, but you feel locked in by financial need. You may have been drawn into a culture of success in an organization and are convinced that the upward movement through levels of reward and prestige are important. In that case, your spirituality has been converted into the corporate ladder, and you may feel controlled by it.

You may have a large view of life and your place in it, but you are working at a job that is so small in scope and insignificant that you can't engage your high ideals. You may want to change the world for the better, but the work you devote forty hours a week to has no relation to your grand ambitions. You may be full of creative ideas but your organization wants you to follow the rules and not make waves.

The spirit can be shackled and crushed by the weight of forces that give you money to live on but no opportunity to make progress with your ambitions and ideals. This crushing of the spirit is another form of depression related to work, and it is commonplace.

You know that Sting's international reputation as an artist

didn't spring into being out of nothing. As he sat there in the government office filling out a mindless form, "Sting" was somewhere in him waiting to emerge. In his reflecting on his early experiences, you sense the frustration and painful anticipation. His spirit was ready to burst into the open, like the winged horse Pegasus leaping from the head of the Medusa, the fearful Gorgon who turned everything in sight to stone.

The Medusa aspect of modern life, its tendency to keep us frozen when our spirits yearn to be liberated and effective, can dominate us all. It frustrates by suppressing the spirit that needs expression. The spirit in us wants a public role. At least it longs for some form of manifestation of who we are. Maybe that yearning is implicated in our cult of celebrity: We get caught in an emotional complex, seeing our own possibility in the grand lives of others.

When it is suppressed in ordinary life, the spirit can reappear in an aggressive form. Many people are angry because the world has broken or imprisoned their spirit. They become aggressive sometimes in small ways and sometimes in tragic forms of violence.

My friend Scottie looks like a very peaceable person, kind and gracious always. But as he talks, I notice that he often tells funny stories that express anger at his family or at his workplace of the moment. You would have to listen closely to appreciate the intensity of his anger, because it is so concealed and wrapped in marvelous humor. Sometimes it scares me.

I know him to be a visionary person. He has many ideas about changing the world and helping people. But it's clear that he hasn't had an opportunity to put those strong feelings into action. I think it would help him if he could find a suitable context for his passions. As it is, his ideals turn into cynicism, and you see the makings of a frustrated, perhaps wasted, life.

The spirit is strong and focused, but it can succumb to the pressures of pragmatism. It can be sacrificed for materialistic purposes, but then it shows up disguised in symptoms you might never expect: rage at your children, neglect of your home (passive-aggressive anger), cynicism, excessive criticism, whining, and withdrawal from life (again, passive-aggressiveness).

Soul and Spirit at Work

When soul and spirit come together creatively, you remain attached to the circumstances of your life—your family, your place, nature, your traditions—and you pursue your ideals. These two directions represent soul and spirit. You appreciate the simple pleasures and your deep connections with people, even as you explore the world in pursuit of your dreams.

But if you are afraid of life's potential and hide out in the place where you grew up or in your family, or if you freeze your spirit in some ideology or belief system, you will have no vibrant soul and spirit to bring to your work. Both soul and spirit have to be alive, or else one will suffer from wounds to the other.

My wife and I went to a cell-phone distributor to update our telephones. A warm, capable—I would say "soulful"—man took care of us. He knew what he was doing, and he connected to us with his heart as well as his skills. He was clearly very concerned to give us just what we needed, and he gave us what turned out to be good advice. But every time he told us about the phones we were purchasing and details of the service, his manager would butt in to make sure we were getting the information we needed. He was constantly undermining his employee's small degree of power and crushing his spirit. It was sad and painful to watch this slow, constant hammering of a man's spirit.

Many people begin their careers full of enthusiasm, caring for their customers and their projects, hoping to achieve great things. Soon, they discover that the real world can place limits on imagination and feeling. A man who was a chef at a good but not extraordinary restaurant in a classy New England town once recounted that the owner threatened to fire him if he gave one more extra cloth napkin to a patron in need of one. It cost too much to launder so many napkins, the manager told him. The chef became frustrated and burned himself badly in an accident at the stove a week later and then quit.

People can be motivated and even excited about their work if their souls are free to connect and the spirits liberated to explore their potential. When they are not so fortunate, they may suffer in either direction: from neglect of soul or the suppression of spirit.

Nurturing Soul and Spirit at Work

Soul is to be found in ordinary life—in the home, family, and neighborhood. It goes deeper into memory, deep emotions, heartfelt connections and attachments, and a deep personal sense of fate and calling. Attention to any of these things can give soul to your work.

But it isn't always easy to nurture these soul elements in a society that is moving in a different direction. Family, neighborhood, and local businesses are almost a thing of the past in many areas, replaced by national and multinational organizations and labels. Large companies continue to swallow small companies. Outsourcing goes on without any sign of slowing down.

It's more difficult to feel connected to a large corporation than to a family business, and so this quality of soul also disappears in the march toward globalization. Many workers find themselves in a workplace that hardly resembles the place where they first started in a job, because the changes brought by the larger corporations often decrease the "personality" of the organization and give the worker fewer signs of history, personality, and tradition, which are all soul qualities.

In many instances it is left to the worker himself to foster qualities of soul. The family photographs, the special plants and flowers, and the knickknacks and other objects that symbolize home and memory and attachment become more significant than ever.

Feelings of belonging, connection, history, and involvement may seem secondary to the person designing and managing the job, but these soul qualities have everything to do with good and fulfilling work. They may appear to be second in importance to productivity and efficiency, and yet they have an impact on the success of the work being done. Tardiness, absenteeism, and sloppy work are often due to the absence of soul in the workplace.

As a person looks for a life work, these qualities truly come to the foreground. By definition a life work is deep-seated and emotional. A person will only feel connected to his life work if his job allows deep emotions, memory, and the love of doing something significant. A worker may feel engaged with his life work because he feels at home in a particular business and devoted to the product. A life work is as much an emotional accomplishment as a concrete achievement.

I mention memory because the past is a major portion of who we are, a part that people don't see. We know our past as no one else does. We carry it with us and feel its influence. It doesn't fully determine who we are, but it is an important factor. It is a large part of the invisible self that accompanies us as we interview for a job or engage in our work. A mixture of good and bad experiences, the past is something we have to deal with as we move into the future.

The spirit moves in a different direction, but it, too, is part of the mysterious accomplishment we call a life work. Spirit may show itself as an intellectual element. Many people enjoy their work because it makes sense and brings their knowledge and intelligence seriously into play. People like a challenge, the need to figure out solutions and solve problems. If their work is mindless, they are hardly going to feel that their life is fulfilled by it.

I had a conversation with our neighbor Paul, who is teaching the teenagers in town how to build a battery-powered car. He is excited by the challenge to get efficiency and speed out of the vehicle and has each young person dedicated to a particular problem. He expects them to rise above their assumption of ignorance in these matters and find out how to solve each problem and make the program work as a whole. Paul's attitude inspires the young people and adds a natural kind of spirit and enthusiasm to the work.

Behind Paul's knowledge and intellectual curiosity is a broader-spirited concern: how to inspire teenagers and keep them focused on a communal project. Paul's work is an example of social action, which is a primary spiritual quality in work. You can see how it fulfills him and contributes to his life work, especially at a time in life when he could be fully retired and just taking care of himself.

Spirit always has a quality of transcendence, some way of going beyond the status quo. You may be building culture, making advancements in science, helping children move into the future, or creating a more ethical and just society. These are all spiritual qualities, insofar as they apply vision and a developed sense of values.

When spiritual aspects of work go unattended, the job becomes too local, too wrapped up in personal need, and makes life too complacent. It is stagnant and only practical. It doesn't move into a better future or engage visionary aspects of living. My neighbor Paul's work has strong qualities of both soul and spirit: It is local and national, amateur and professional, engaging only a few local teenagers and yet an example for a nation in need of inspiration.

The natural world, too, has a spiritual aspect, as it offers its profound mysteries for our contemplation and awes us with its vastness and powers. Some jobs fulfill the spirit simply by being so closely associated with nature, such as a position in a national park, cleaning up a river or lake, or forecasting the weather. Other work could borrow some spirit from nature: A company could make the natural world part of the factory or corporate headquarters. I once gave a lecture in a courtroom in the city of Limerick, Ireland. The building faced the Shannon River and the room we were in had a large window opening to the river, allowing the proceedings indoors to have indirect access to that important natural feature of the city. The architect who designed that room had addressed the spiritual needs of the citizens in a simple and concrete manner.

Any work environment could be a more spiritual place through architecture—some buildings are more transcendent than others. The schedule could also include opportunities for meditation, prayer, and social service. An empty room for personal retreat, a cabinet for collecting used clothing for distribution, or paintings and statuary representing the spiritual traditions of the world would all add to the spiritual atmosphere of the workplace.

These spiritual qualities of the workplace have their counterparts in the psychology of the person in search of a life work. You need to meditate on your endeavor. You can retreat into nature for inspiration. You can draw on the spiritual literature of the world.

You can surround yourself with artwork of quality and intelligence. You can engage in social service as a way of finding yourself in the world around you.

Soul and spirit work like siblings or lovers to vivify and inspire the quest for a life work. Together, they offer depth and transcendence, memory and hope, intimacy and universality. They engage the whole person in the process of creating, over a lifetime, a work life that satisfies and offers a sense of meaning. These two dimensions make for a complete experience of work and, in the end, give your life work the great dimensions it needs to fulfill you as a person in a family and community and engaged with the world.

Spirit moves us into the future, while the soul keeps us tied to the past. Both are rich resources, and in the pages that follow we will see how these two factors, the very deep and the transcendent, give dimension to our quest for a life work. After all, we are not just looking for a job, but rather an activity that will make our lives make sense.

CHAPTER FOUR

RECONCILING WITH
THE PAST

*Leonardo advised aspiring artists to discover the pictures to be
found in cracks in walls; Chinese sages were conceived as their
mothers stepped into the footprints of unicorns; all of us make
up our lives out of the cracks in the walls of our past
memories and the unicorn footprints of our futures.*

LYNDA SEXSON

hen we want to get on with the alchemy of our life
work, we might look into the vessel that holds the
raw material of our lives. In it we can find our painful
memories: people who got in the way, experiments that failed,
hopes and promises that didn't work out, losses and failures, rejec-
tions and interrupted careers.

All of this "bad" stuff from the past is like compost. We have to
go and gather it and place it in the pile that will be the dark resource
for the alchemy about to take place. Jung said that if you don't have
a pile of rotten stuff to work with, you should go out and get some.
Most of us don't have to look far. We are painfully aware of the

many dark moments in our work history and our problem is more an unwillingness to dredge it up and look at it once again than to have an empty pot.

Alchemists referred to this phase of the Work as *nigredo*, the blackening. In the laboratory lengthy and strong heat has given the mass of material in the vessels a dark, and perhaps even charred, appearance. Metaphorically, the material of our life, subjected now to the heat of anxious consideration, memory, and analysis, shows its darkness and shadow, its bitterness and sadness.

This is the time to watch all those old memories turn various shades of dark as we feel their bitter emotions and remember their discouraging influences. As you can imagine, alchemy was a smelly business, and as you go about the alchemy of your own life, you can catch the stench of bad memories.

All of this bothersome business is appropriate and useful. Telling your unhappy stories, calling up memories you might rather leave untouched, and remembering people who didn't help you much on your way is all valuable—your bad experiences are as much a part of you as the good ones, and to be fully present to your current work, you have to include them as well. This is only a phase—later your focus will shift to brighter ground. But you can't omit the *nigredo* out of some sentimental focus on the bright side of things. If you do refuse the darker material, the alchemy will never truly get under way.

Failure

Memories of childhood and family lie deep in a person's psyche, and failures from the past also play a strong role in the unfolding of a life work. Over time, you create a history that becomes your narrative, a string of jobs and positions that create your identity. For most of us, that history is full of missteps, lost opportunities, and crushing failures.

Some people are able to brush off the mistakes and persevere in their careers with some optimism, but many people so identify with their failures that they develop a negative image of themselves and expect to fail at whatever they do. There doesn't seem to be a particle of optimism in my friend Scottie's head. He has identified with failure, and the spurts of hope at the start of a new job have become part of his story of failure.

For some, the impact of failure is linked to a parent harshly forbidding them never to fail. You would think that parents would understand the importance of supporting their children and guiding them through difficulties and failures, but in therapy I hear story after story of a demanding, hysterical, or otherwise overpowering parent. With strident warnings sharp in their memories, some people can't imagine taking a risk at work and perhaps courting failure.

The damning risk of failure can meet you at every turn. You can be successful in your work and be known for your competence and past brilliance. Then, when you fail, people may be shocked, and their displeasure may persuade you not to take any more chances. Successful people can reach a plateau where the fear of failure inhibits them and keeps them stuck at their current level.

My own life story contains a special genre of failure. When I was living in a religious order and preparing to be a priest, I was studying theology at the monastery but also pursuing my interest in music composition at a local university. My music studies were part-time and secondary to theology.

I did quite well for a couple of years, and then I met a professor who offered to lead me in an independent study in composition. He was a brilliant, well-read, amazingly gifted man, one of the few true geniuses I have met in my life, and his knowledge extended far beyond music. As a composer he was brilliant, but he was also gifted at languages.

At first, he gave me some basic instructions on how to create a coherent piece of music. Together we analyzed old scores and listened to the latest styles. Soon he was asking me to write full pieces for piano or voice or ensemble. It wasn't easy for me to do all that he demanded—I was taking a full course of theological studies, some taught in Latin, at the same time. I now understand that the limits on my time made it difficult for me to excel in music. But I was also intimidated by this man's talent. He could do so much in music naturally, without effort, that I began to believe that, given my lesser talent, I would always be a second-rate composer if I pursued my goals. Eventually I left music behind, after two university degrees and many years devoted to the study.

Years later, I wondered if I made a good decision in abandoning a career in music. I know that I could have done good work in schools by teaching, conducting, and arranging. Today I get satisfaction from playing the piano daily and arranging music for university and professional choirs, but I still wonder if I could have had a good career in music. The regret is not very strong, but it does bring some tension to my life as a writer, even though I feel strongly called to that work.

The tension I feel about a lost music career feels positive to me. It keeps me on edge, questioning myself in a constructive way, even though the feelings themselves are not pleasant. Whenever I read of people who have managed to sustain several careers at once, I wish I could have done it. But then I'm placed back in the vessel of my calling. I want to crawl out of it sometimes, but it is who I am. The tension keeps me alive, and the knowledge that I am doing my life work by writing eases my heart.

The Relentless Dog of History

Even if you are successful at a job, if you have had an especially difficult history, you will feel its effects throughout your life. This isn't to say that you can't be happy or make progress with the weight of your past, but you may never be fully free of it. It may always nag at you and haunt you.

When we talk about a life work, we are not imagining perfection. You may find work that satisfies your cravings, but you may also, at the same time, continue to feel the effects of a difficult childhood, abuse, and failure. The amazingly successful and self-possessed Oprah Winfrey confesses that she still suffers the effects of early years of abuse and poverty. In her, though, you can see her past suffering as a strength, allowing her to keep her sense of values in the midst of wealth and fame and to use her resources with generosity and imagination.

I have a friend, Steven, who grew up in a tough south Boston neighborhood in a hardworking but in many ways ill-functioning family. All his life he has been doing real grunt work in the family business of cleaning banks, offices, and restaurants after hours.

I first met Steven when I was teaching art therapists. He stood out from the crowd with his intelligence, good humor, and talent. He was a dancer, actor, and director. Eventually he went off to get a Ph.D.—he is interested in psychology, philosophy, theater, and a number of other fields. While writing his dissertation, he lived with my family for a year and a half. It was a sad day for us all when he went back home to help his brother carry on the family business.

I was a member of Steven's dissertation committee, and I was overwhelmed by the sheer intelligence and insight in his work. He continues to direct plays, teach drama to young people, and apply his many ideas about culture as he keeps theater alive in his small seacoast town.

I don't know if Steven has found his life work. I think he is certainly well on the way. Yet he seems to carry his south Boston experience with him in everything he does. He has gaps here and there, the burden of his past, and yet he has done more than most to raise the level of culture in his community. To me, he is an example of someone who doesn't try to completely overcome his past and yet carves out a productive, influential, highly intelligent life work. He embodies James Hillman's idea of a person fired up with his own calling and going strongly in his own direction, irrespective of family pressures and problems. The dark influences are there, but they don't put out the flame of his creative intelligence.

My family and I tell him: "Stop cleaning restrooms. Make some good money. You've got a Ph.D. now, get a teaching job." But all this well-intentioned cheerleading is off the mark. Steven knows who he is and what he must do. Somehow his necessity to help with the family business is part of his life work, at least up to now. He follows his own urgings and certainly knows better than we do what is driving him toward fulfillment.

A life work is a multicolored, tattered quilt. It is not a simple, monochromatic, one-size-fits-all template that you simply adjust to. It may have gaps and holes and incomplete sections. It may not even feel like a life work, especially when you are in the middle of it. There may come a time when you can look back and see the sense in all the parts and glimpse a true life work, but even then it may be full of holes made by a long history of struggles.

You don't have to look for perfection. Dark shadows from the past may always color what you are doing. You don't have to expect that one day you will resolve your family, your childhood, and the ups and downs of your life. A life work is more a sensation than a fact, a realization that your work has been meaningful and not that it has finally become complete and flawless.

The Good That Can Come from Bad Influences

When you look at the life stories of successful people, you notice that many of them had negative elements in their past. They didn't spring up from well-intentioned, wise, farsighted parents and social settings. Nor did they always "overcome" their past, fighting against negative influences and succeeding in spite of interfering relatives. Sometimes what appears to be a negative influence turns out to be a positive push forward.

Dr. Jonas Salk, the famous researcher whose work on a polio vaccine was one of those rare accomplishments that in a single stroke saves lives, came from a family of Russian immigrants without much education. As a youth, Salk knew he wanted to do something to help humankind, and he seriously considered becoming a lawyer and then a politician. But his mother had little confidence in this idea. "My mother didn't think I would make a very good lawyer," he said, reflecting on the turn of events that led to his career in medicine. "And I believe that her reasons were that I couldn't really win an argument with her."

Salk didn't consider his mother an obstacle. On the contrary, he felt encouraged by her generally. You may wonder about a highly intelligent, thoughtful man making a life decision based on his mother's belief that if he couldn't argue with her, he couldn't deal with a court. But sometimes negative comments lead to positive decisions. Maybe she knew her son well and had a vision of his future that was hidden in her simple comment on his ability to argue.

Parents can steer a child forward toward a life calling in both negative and positive ways. A child can process what he hears, whether it's supportive or challenging. In the long run, it might be better for a parent to speak his mind, so long as he isn't being just blindly critical for neurotic reasons, and let the child work out a life for himself. Jonas Salk said that he had two general principles in mind as he grew up: He wanted to foster his innate sense of wonder, and he wanted to make a contribution to humanity. These spiritual ideas kept him going as he sorted out the best particular route to follow. He could digest his mother's ideas in light of those principles.

The Pulitzer Prize–winning trumpeter Wynton Marsalis grew up on the streets in New Orleans. His mother was "very smart," he says, and made him read when he was a child. His father was a musician who gave his son a trumpet when he was six, but he wasn't interested at first and didn't start playing until he was twelve. His father also treated his children like adults. "And my father, he would always talk to us like we were grown men, just in the content of his conversations. We never knew what he was talking about half the time. We'd just go, 'Yeah, yeah, okay.' Like you could ask daddy just something basic, 'Daddy, can I have a dollar?' And he would go into like a discussion!"[1]

Children may wonder what their parents are talking about when they speak to them in adult rather than child language, but eventually the vision of the parent may pay off. Wynton Marsalis describes a childhood of mild delinquency and a slow development. Eventually he became an intelligent musician and a highly cultured man, a major influence on other young people trying to make it in a confusing world.

As an adult, Wynton Marsalis understands that though his father's music was not the kind he could pursue specifically, it taught him in more general ways how to be a good artist and develop the character needed to practice and to deal with adversity.

What you do with your past is more important than what it threatens to do to you. You have to see what is valuable in it, shape it to your own hopes and principles, and not get overwhelmed with its negative elements. The past, good and bad, is a rich resource as you try to find your life work. You may think you have to focus on the future to find your career, whereas you may find more material, the alchemical *prima materia*, in your childhood and family.

What Not to Do with the Past

Your past is who you are. It is your particular fate. You may wish it had been different, but it is what it is. It is your starting point and the place you always go back to in memory. You carry it with you.

For most people, the past is a mixture of blessings and trouble. I remember my kind and generous grandmother once telling me that she would rather not have been born than to raise a family in the depression era. Because the past can be a heavy burden and can understandably affect present attitudes, you may be tempted to deal with it heavy-handedly.

Some people take the heroic approach. They are going to overcome their past and be successful in spite of it. They put their energy into not being something rather than in being someone unique. The singer Johnny Cash once expressed his philosophy about the past: "You build on failure. You use it as a stepping stone. Close the door on the past. You don't try to forget the mistakes, but you don't dwell on it. You don't let it have any of your energy, or any of your time, or any of your space. If you analyze it as you're moving forward, you'll never fall in the same trap twice." He says you should close the door on the past, but then he adds that you should analyze it so you don't repeat mistakes. So, he really means, you don't close the door.[2]

Some blame certain people in their past for their failure to find the work they want. They may blame a parent for not giving them support, a teacher for not understanding them, or a friend for not giving them good advice. I used to blame my music composition teacher for not preparing me sufficiently for graduate work, but I was lucky to have had him as a teacher for a few years. It was my choice not to enter fully into a career in music.

Blaming is a defensive maneuver. It helps you to avoid facing yourself and your choices. It's different from analysis, where you carefully sort out the reasons for your progress or lack of it. It's one thing to tell the story of your father not appreciating your world and the desires you have; it's another to examine his background and come to an understanding of the differences between you.

The past is not a problem to be solved. It's your mystery, the complicated tale of who you are and how you came to this point in your life. You may analyze your personal history, but analysis is different from problem solving. As you analyze your development, you may gain insight, but you will never fully grasp how you came to be. Analysis is ongoing and always unfinished; a problem is solved once and for all.

Many people look at themselves and their lives as problems. They are always looking for a clue that will explain everything and finally make life better. In therapy, I have met many people who are looking for the final solution to their lives. If all they find in therapy is insight and deepening, they move on to the next therapist, hoping that he or she will possess the ultimate clue to their lives.

A woman once came to me asking help in finding a direction

in life. "I want to do something with my life," she said. Then she told me how she had married the CEO of the corporation she worked for. She had money, friends, and possessions, but she felt deeply unsatisfied. She hated her marriage most of all. It just didn't work out, but she didn't want the mess of a divorce. She particularly didn't want to appear as a failure in the eyes of her friends and family.

I reflected back to her the intensity of her displeasure in her marriage, suggesting that dealing with her feelings and her life at this point would be a good place to start. But she wanted an immediate solution to her career woes. We talked for a while, feeling the stalemate, and one day she announced that she was leaving the bad marriage. Suddenly her life began to open up. She developed a new group of friends, discovered that her family was relieved to see her finally released from the marriage, and eventually found an entirely new area of work.

In this woman's case, a period of thoughtful consideration of her marriage and her family led to the career vision that had eluded her for a long time. She had to reflect on her past, not overcoming it but seeing more clearly. Establishing a new relationship to her past decisions and her views about her family effected a powerful catharsis, a clearing of her vision. Then she was able to move forward. She didn't try to change her past or overcome it, but only have a deeper understanding of it.

The past feels like a burden only when it is thick, solid, and unsorted. You repeat the same stories, blame the same people, and feel the same frustrations. If you can look more closely and tell the stories with new detail and insight, the past loosens up. You see it in slightly fresh ways, and it is no longer a bothersome lump of emotion. It can become lighter to carry and even offer support for a new career, where before it was only an obstacle.

You don't have to be a genius at interpretation, but you do have to tell your stories openly and allow any insight to come forward. It helps to find the right people to listen attentively to your stories. A good listener is sometimes difficult to find. Most people are too quick with advice or they side too readily with your biases and interpretations. When you do find someone who will listen thoughtfully to your stories, tell them with the hope for fresh understanding. In the next chapter, you will be given specific lessons in storytelling.

One of the richest insights in alchemy is the idea that you have "stuff" to work with. You don't have to go into a blank future empty-handed; you can sort through the positive and negative elements of your past. Alchemists said that the *prima materia,* the raw stuff of your life, may contain a great deal of rejected, unpromising, and even objectionable material. But out of it, and in spite of its confusion, you can make a satisfying life.

We are going to move on now to another aspect of that raw material—its tendency to present itself as chaotic and unformed. Everyone would like a clear message about what to do next in life, but usually we have chaos, with, at best, hints of where to turn. A philosophy of chaos might help as, one time after another, we have to deal with confusion rather than order.

CHAPTER FIVE

CREATIVE CHAOS

Trust thyself: every heart vibrates to that iron string. Accept the
place the divine providence has found for you, the society of
your contemporaries, the connection of events.

RALPH WALDO EMERSON

The alchemist sits in the quiet of his oratory and prays and
reflects on the long process of doing his work and pursuing his elusive goal. He is patient and observant, peering
into exotic glass vessels, watching intensely every change in color
and texture. He begins in ignorance and aware that chaos marks the
beginning of the process. But he thinks of chaos as a good thing, as
a beginning state full of promise.

The great fifteenth-century philosopher Nicholas of Cusa said
of this opening condition of chaos, "It has no name, though it is
sometimes called various things: Matter, Chaos, Possibility, Being-
Able-to-Develop or Underlying."[1]

You sit with the chaos of your work life, perhaps not able to
get a useful job, certainly far from feeling that you have your life
work in your hands. You sit there with your failures, wrong turns,

bad choices, incomplete projects, far-off dreams, and frustrating expectations—any life teems with raw material, and it takes a long time to do the inventory. You sense the chaos and want to do something about it. You may not see your situation as one of possibility and the ability to develop, but if you trust the alchemical wisdom you may glimpse the secret of the chaotic. It allows change and development, whereas a clear and fixed job or position might blind you to future possibility. You may be too comfortable outside of chaos to consider possible alternatives.

A good beginning step in looking for your life work, then, is a quiet one. You take in all your frustrations, your painful history, and your influences, and you look at who and what you are. The first phase is observation, knowing the stuff of which you're made and where you're coming from. You get to know yourself and your world better than you have ever known them, and that knowledge allows you to step into the future.

After getting in touch with your soul, your essential vitality, and then considering your roots and your past experiences, you may be ready for the chaos. If you didn't have chaos in your life, you might be superficially happy with your job, but you wouldn't have the impetus to consider your deep desire for a life work. It might make all the difference to understand that chaos, though disturbing, is a positive thing.

Prima Materia, *or Your Raw Material*

The people I have mentioned who are painfully in search of the right work, I would like to take away on a retreat. The first day we would do nothing but consider basic issues. We would set aside career options and training. I would ask: Who are you? Where do you come from? What were your ancestors and your parents like? What sorts of emotions are now stirring in you? In particular, what are your desires and your fears? This is the start of the process. You begin with the basic raw material and gradually make your way to the practical life.

The point in turning to memory is to enter more fully in imagination into the obstacles to your work life. Today people want to minimize their discomfort, but ultimately a little pain is not a bad price for discovering more about the factors that are blocking you.

In therapy I have witnessed many people searching for deeper satisfaction in their lives, but they are so identified with the future, with possibilities that bounce in their heads and give them pleasure for the moment, that they don't really know what they want, or better, what their heart wants. Finding a life work is all about desire, not a passing wish—a deep, long-standing desire to be someone and to do something. Yet people often do not know themselves well enough to know what they want.

I have always appreciated alchemy as a model for self-examination because it offers a picture of someone looking at a pile of chaotic, unformed material. With an alchemical psychology, we don't look at ourselves, as if in a mirror, but at the material that makes up our past and present. The alchemist zeroes in on the stuff he has put into the vessel; we can focus, too, on the material that has poured into us over the years, making us into who we are. This way we can see more of what is actually there as opposed to what we would like to see.

You look and you see chaos. Nothing fits. Nothing stands out. There is no order and no sign of anything significant for the future. But that is the way it should be at the beginning. The feeling of chaos is not comfortable, but I assure you that it is promising.

Chaos is pure possibility, with no clear goals and directions to get in the way.

In the case of therapy, people usually arrive in a state of chaos. They rarely call and say they need therapy because everything is in order and life is going as expected. They are motivated to tend their souls precisely because they feel the chaos. Chaos is not just the state of life's disarray; it is the emotion of unsettledness and confusion. Alchemists referred to this opening conditon as *massa confusa*, a term that hardly needs translation. We could call it "a big mess."

My friend Scottie is clearly in chaos, with many parts of his life threatening to fall apart. But he isn't in tune with his chaos. He keeps trying to keep it at bay by not allowing any time to pass between one failed job and the other. As far I can see, he won't sit down and look at the stuff of his life. He is "acting out" the chaos by rushing blindly from one place to another, rather than facing it and dealing with it directly. He himself is chaotic, when it might be better for him to stand back and consider the chaotic stuff of his life—his unhappy job, his stressful family, his threatened marriage, his alcoholism, and his depression.

Find Good Vessels

How do you deal with the chaos of a work life yet to be formed? A contemporary way to do what the alchemists did—place all the stuff, good and bad, in a glass vessel—is to find a container, a vessel of some sort, that will hold your chaos. Therapy is such a vessel. But there are many others. A friendship, a family, a community, a church, a club, a conversation, a diary, a dinner, a walk with someone—these can all serve as vessels for the stuff that plagues you

as you desperately look for your life work. Within all these contain-
ers is one of the most effective vessels: your stories.

The stuff of your emotions, memories, and hopes appears in the
stories you tell, and so it is important to tell your stories openly, completely, and with feeling. For that you need a friend or even a professional counselor who can listen closely to what you have to say.

Stories are not the same as explanations and interpretations.
People often say what is wrong with their lives or offer various reasons why they feel stuck. But these ideas may be part of the problem, because they may be shaped by the very attitudes that are
getting in the way.

Stories are different. They are more neutral, in the sense that
they can be read in different ways. They are not so self-conscious,
when they are told just as stories. In the telling you may add details
that surprise you and give the listener insights.

Telling your stories can be a pleasure. The story form itself is
more satisfying to most people, compared to analysis and interpretation. People enjoy telling and listening to stories, and this element
of pleasure is an important one as you go deeper into the process of
exploring your roots and discovering a life work.

You can begin your storytelling at the beginning, with your
early memories, and go from there. Or, you could begin with stories about what is going on now. You shouldn't neglect a story that
comes to you because it seems irrelevant—you may discover its rel-
evance much later.

As you speak, your stories show you that your chaos is not just
an unidentifiable mass, a glob of confusion. It is made up of particular things. Certain people are central, certain events more significant than others, certain feelings consistent. Your stories, without
interpretation, already give you the beginnings of order. They help
you sort through the mess, and sorting through is a major first step.

Alchemists called this initial stage *solutio*. It's interesting that the English word *solution* has two meanings: solving a problem or dissolving something in a liquid. Chemistry speaks of a substance being "in solution." Alchemy uses the word in two senses. *Solutio* can mean "in solution," dissolving in a liquid, but it also has the darker meaning of things coming apart.

As we sort out our past and current emotions and struggles, we may find this dissolving or sorting out to be a painful process. We might be tempted to leave out the stories that are painful to recall. But the process of alchemy requires that we have a courageous heart and sort out all the things that have gone into our experience up to this point.

Telling the stories of your life not only offers you a vessel for the chaos, it also provides you with a useful means of sorting out your life. But there are good stories and bad stories, effective ways of recounting your history and clever—but ultimately pointless—ways of avoiding the bad stuff.

Telling your stories well is not a given talent. A story can prematurely impose a meaning where chaos still reigns. It can rush to a conclusion that is not truly felt. It can give the illusion of meaning where meaning is not in sight.

I have a neighbor, Tom, who has been successful at his work. He makes a good living doing many of the things he likes to do, but he still feels incomplete and unhappy with his current job as a human resources director in a large corporation. The impersonal atmosphere at work seems to be his main problem and currently he has a strong desire to find a more entrepreneurial job, as he puts it.

The corporation he works for is good at allowing him some independence and creative thought, but his need for self-expression is so strong that he feels uncomfortably confined. He has many ideas about what he can do for society, how he can best use his time, and how to "package" his message. He is an attractive, bright, articulate man. You get the sense that he could be successful in whatever project he took up.

When I ask about his discontent, he begins talking about his father and brothers. "I'm still trying to please my father," he jokes. But it is no joke, of course. Many people are still trying to justify their lives in the eyes of their parents, and the weight of the family's experience of work often drags down the children. If the family members were successful, there is the challenge to be at least equally good at what you do. If they were largely failures, then you have to shake off that inheritance. Between these extremes lie all the complicated values and personality issues that emit from the family and affect the ideas and experiments of the children and grandchildren.

As Tom talks about his work life, he begins by saying how supportive his family had been, but as his story gets into full gear, gaps begin to appear. (One of the primary dictionary meanings of *chaos* is "gap.") As he goes on, the story becomes truer and the chaos more manifest. A person telling his story doesn't always break through so easily to the underlying chaos.

One of my primary tasks as a therapist is to help people tell their stories, for storytelling is an art, in both the aesthetic sense and the alchemical sense. You tell a story well by giving it a shape and dynamics, but you also tell a story so that your heart is moved by it, and your thoughts go deeper and your emotions emerge. If we unleash the chaos early in the therapy, I feel that the work is progressing well.

Aids for Telling Your Story

Over the years I have developed a few simple aids that may help a person examine her past or aid her in counseling a friend going through a crisis about work. The purpose of these simple rules is to keep the story open and honest, loyal to any fruitful chaos that might be present, and alert to any conscious or unconscious efforts to make the story sound better than it really is.

First, I give a person the opportunity and the space to remember. Most of us are too busy to take time out to remember in any serious way. I invite a client to tell her stories, and I listen without interfering. Here is where the Eastern principle of "not doing" is crucial. Listening begins in not doing things that may seem logical, intuitive, and helpful—clarifying, interpreting, and giving advice. I have to remind myself not to interfere or interrupt, even if I'm struck by a magnificent intuition or interpretation. The story being told deserves respect.

To be fully engaged in your present life, you have to take the past in and own it and feel it with all its intensity. If you distance yourself from it, ever so slightly, it will become an obstacle, something you refuse to make part of yourself. You may be uncomfortable looking at it closely, but there is also a satisfaction to be had from absorbing it—a simple pleasure in self-discovery. If you don't make it part of yourself, it will be there anyway, influencing you subliminally, and generally for the bad. You may continue to act out past patterns or rebel against past assaults.

The past may not be pretty, but it is who you are, and if you are going to progress into a better future you have to be honest with yourself about where you are coming from. It has brought you to this moment, and your choices now depend on how you relate to it. Are you going to acknowledge it and go on, or are you going to avoid it and remain stuck?

Tom seems to have had a catharsis simply by realizing that his family background is a factor in his discontent. When I first tell him that I'm interested in hearing about his family background, I can see skepticism in his face. But once he gets on with his stories, his eyes open up and the doubts go away. He warms up to the stories and obviously takes some significant insights from them.

Apparently he hadn't considered that as an adult he was still living partly in the family mythology—the assumptions, values, and ways of seeing the world that he had grown up with. He may have had his opinions about his mother, father, and brothers, but now he begins to see them less as concrete people and more as characters in his own story.

People are often not in the habit of seeing through to deeper layers in the stories they tell or hear. They take in the details and then want to consider some action. But the first telling of a story may be just a sketch. You have to tell it again and again, because it gets richer, deeper, and perhaps darker with each telling. You can expand on certain details that draw your attention or cause you to feel anxious or just interested.

In therapy, after a client completes her story, I may ask her to tell it again or to expand on certain parts that seem fruitful. This is not the same as satisfying curiosity about details. If a woman tells about an embarrassing encounter with a former lover, and I ask, "Where did this take place?" I may only be satisfying some inane curiosity of my own, instead of zeroing in on the substance of the story, the emotional meeting.

Curiosity is one thing; therapeutic listening is another. Something she said may strike me as being relevant to a current life problem, or I may sense some unease in the telling and assume that there is some emotional potency in that area. I'm trying to intensify the experience of the past rather than soften or mute it.

As you explore your memories, you can always delve deeper. Think of your past as one story embedded in another or many levels of events. You can do an archaeology of your own past, digging away at debris and going deeper and deeper until an insight sparkles like a vein of gold deep in the dark stuff of your history. A quaint image from alchemy shows two men digging in the earth like miners searching for valuable material buried there. Mining your past is another way of doing alchemy.

"Digging up the past" may not seem very attractive. Maybe "mining the past for nuggets of gold" is better. When you are looking for valuable ore, you are not just digging up facts. The fascinating thing about stories of the past is that they usually say something enlightening about the present. I remember that my father was a teacher, and suddenly I realize that I am part of a lineage. Teaching is not just a whim of mine; I've inherited it. It has roots. It is bigger than me.

I find that people reach a point in the descent into their story where they think they have gone as far as possible. But I encourage them to delve deeper and explore areas that may not seem significant or may be somewhat frightening or repugnant. This step into new territory almost always offers helpful realizations.

I was once working in therapy with a young man who was living in a ménage à trois with two women. One of them was strong and very forceful, the other meek and quiet. He enjoyed the complex relationship generally, but he also felt that he was too subservient and often taken advantage of. Previously, he had told me about his mother, who, when he was a child, used to sleep in most mornings, depressed and unable to enter actively into life. One day I asked him to repeat that story about his mother, and this time he added the detail that his father always made breakfast for his mother and served it to her in bed. It was a small thing, but it led to a deep conversation about the power issues between men and women, a theme at the heart of his unusual home life.

A third technique is to notice resistance to a memory. You may end your story abruptly, hesitant to continue. You may skip over certain details or dismiss them with a remark like, "It isn't necessary to talk about that." Sometimes people are more direct: "This is something I've never been able to talk about."

When I perceive resistance to memory in a client who really wants to explore himself, I don't push it at the moment or try to force a confession. I'm patient and over time offer opportunities to open up. Usually patience pays off, because the story truly wants to be told. Archaeologists are patient people.

Resistance is subtle and often doesn't look like defensiveness: You may feel suddenly tired. You remember something you have to do urgently. You decide it would be better to pursue this line of thought at another time. At the same time, you may feel that there is a story in you that wants to be told. I have never felt that a person should tell everything and aim for absolute disclosure. Some stories may never be told. But usually resistance is due to fear, and it would be useful to take some steps toward revealing a story that is difficult to tell.

As you tell your stories, especially those you have kept hidden for a long time, insights about your past and your character come out. You get to know yourself better and are then better equipped to make decisions. The release of a hidden story expands your understanding.

My client who lived in the ménage à trois, after being surprised at the memory of his father serving his mother, felt a strong need to delve more deeply into that story and other related ones. He had started his own business and found that he had similar problems at home and at work: He was too passive and compliant with customers and with his housemates. The stories of his parents helped him explore this crucial aspect of his character.

Anyone can employ these three simple techniques for thinking about the influence of the past. You can give yourself opportunities to tell your story plainly and openly, without interpretations or resolutions for improvement. You can tell it again and again and notice how in the retelling details emerge that have some poignancy to them. The further unfolding of your story is a step in the right direction.

Finally, you can catch yourself in resistance to parts of your story. You can notice omissions, hesitancy, or a tendency to gloss over certain details. It isn't easy to spot your own interference, and so a good friend being an active listener can be useful, especially when you need encouragement to face painful memories. Eventually, you may so appreciate the positive value of chaos in your unfolding work life that you will want to search for it and make sure it's revealed in your storytelling.

Sometimes people simply generalize, when a particular detail is necessary to make the necessary breakthrough. A person will say, "Yes, my family didn't give me much support when I was in school." The story is, "My father wanted me to go into the business he had started and was disappointed to see me heading toward the arts." Any good story is concrete, including the stories we tell to reconnect with the past.

Telling the stories of the past is a way to be closely in touch with the obstacles that stand in the way of the opus. Rather than escape into pleasant fantasies of a successful future, it may be more useful to gather the courage to face the past in all its disturbing detail.

Of course, it's also important to talk about the present: how you feel now, what is going on in your life, and the hopes and fears affecting you. The present chaos is a rich resource.

Telling your story is a powerful way to bring yourself to the edge of your reality, where you are fully present to your emotions and thoughts and can progress from there with all of your resources.

You hear yourself talking and hear things you didn't notice in the privacy of your own thoughts. You see the reaction of the person listening to you. You have a connection with that person, who can help you clarify your thoughts and hold your emotions. Few things in life are as precious as the opportunity to tell your story with an open heart to a friend or kindhearted stranger.

The Way of Imagination

What is it about failing and making bad decisions that places life on a good course? One answer has to do with the tiny capacity of the human mind. Technically it is vast and complicated, of course, but in relation to the infinite possibilities in life, it is minuscule and no match for life's richness and unpredictability.

We tend to interpret our experiences the way our family has always done it, or the way the culture in which we live does it. Or we have our own prejudices and habits of thought that limit what we see and experience. People often assume that they are always experiencing an objective reality, when in truth they are always seeing through the lens of the familiar stories by which they live.

We deal with the threat of chaos by imposing a known order on it, and that order is usually habitual, ingrained, and defensive. It protects a person from dealing with the new and the unexpected. Bad decisions usually stem from the failure to see the full expanse of life in front of us. Our habits of interpretation are like blinders.

Sometimes a job or career runs into trouble because it is a bad fit, but often we fail because our imaginations can't grasp the richness of the possibilities. Especially at times of big decision making, our attention may be focused too narrowly. Our understanding of the way life works is limited, until we make enough mistakes to know better. But there are never enough mistakes to equal the possibilities.

In failing, we get to know new territory. We're forced to consider options that we never had to imagine before because everything was settled and the future clear. Now, with failure, we have to picture a wide range of options. We may be doing all this in a state of anxiety, but the imagination opens up nevertheless.

Scottie took a job selling cars, but he quickly discovered that he had absolutely no gift for sales and little interest in it. He did a terrible job and within a few weeks was asked to leave. Naturally, he felt bad about being fired, but at least he knew that sales would never be his slot in life. He learned the hard way, but he picked up a valuable lesson. Then his imagination went back to his own field, and he brought new energy to finding a better place in a work area that he knew.

Failure is often the cause of a new chaotic period in life, and if you can appreciate the alchemist's view of chaos, in spite of the pain involved, new possibilities come with the confusion. Chaos is fertile, and failure may be the mother of the chaos.

Admittedly, the emotions surrounding failure may be so strong and so negative that it may seem naive and Pollyanna-like to see the creative element. But human beings can feel and do several things at once. You can be overwhelmed by the negativity of the failure and still have the imagination to see opportunity.

A person of imagination is not undone by the overwhelming weight of facts and feelings. The imagination can penetrate through such things, but to do so a few basic strengths have to be in place.

The imagination is similar to a muscle in the body: It works more effectively, especially against the odds, when it has been practiced, exercised, and honed. Throughout life, even when no work crisis is looming, you can use your imagination habitually, seeing possibilities when the facts suggest otherwise.

My neighbor Tom is always ready with a new idea. Now he finds himself in a job that pays well and gives him security. These two benefits are not only enviable rewards; for many people they would be blocks to further progress. Many people keep their imagination of alternative work shut down so as not to disturb a good salary and financial security.

But Tom's spirit is strong and his imagination unusually alive. He sees through the security to his feelings of discontent, and he can picture himself in a position that will still give him the money he needs, if not the security, and yet answer his yearning for an entrepreneurial style of work.

He is uneasy, of course, about taking the leap out of a secure position, but his sheer ability to picture a more satisfying work situation sustains him. He is taking his time checking out the realistic issues involved in his dreams, but slowly he is moving in the direction in which his spirit wants him to go.

You have to trust your imagination, even when other people are advising you to stay your course and when the facts of your situation stand in front of you like huge granite obstacles. Imagination has the power to break through formidable walls, but you have to allow it its force.

Inspiration Empowers Imagination

You can educate and train your imagination through careful reading. Biographies of successful people can inspire you by giving you models, since most well-known leaders have had to overcome obstacles you might never face.

Biography is a special form of literature in which you can picture yourself, either as you are or as you would like to be. You may identify with the person you're reading about or you may realize what you don't want to be.

Reading about the lives of others need not be so personal and practical. It can also help you develop a philosophy of life by giving you a larger and varied sense of what it means to be a human being. Extraordinary people show how wide the range of human possibility is.

My personal philosophy of life owes a great deal to the lives of Ralph Waldo Emerson, who demonstrates how to be a spiritual leader without being confined to a particular institution or religion; Emily Dickinson, who had the courage and imagination to create an eccentric lifestyle that represented her ideas and values; and even the Marquis de Sade, who risked imprisonment and the disdain of society to express his dark vision with the purpose of offering insight into the human tendency toward evil. Many other biographies stick in my mind and come to me when I am facing some special challenge. I remember that the most creative people find unexpected solutions to ordinary problems.

For me, it has also been important to continue to read certain spiritual and psychological books over and over: the Gospels, the poems of William Blake, the Tao Te Ching, the writings of C. G. Jung and James Hillman, Marsilio Ficino, Anne Sexton, Sufi poets, Samuel Beckett, Oscar Wilde. I find the classic texts and writers more useful than contemporary ones, at least as the foundation for other reading.

Inspiring examples of colorful lives and words of wisdom and encouragement can empower the imagination, making it more of a factor in your decision about your life work. You see the various directions people have gone in their careers. You gain insight into your blocks by seeing how they dealt with theirs. You get encouragement when you see how low they have sunk and yet have ultimately succeeded.

Seeking out solid and useful inspiration is part of the art, an aspect of the alchemy by which your hidden creative self emerges. Of course, inspirational literature and teaching may be nothing but platitudes and shallow truisms that comfort more than inspire, but that doesn't mean that inspiration itself is always superficial.

The word *inspire* means "to breathe into" and brings us back to the idea that to be alive in body and soul means to breathe in and out. An inspiring example gets you breathing again and ready to approach your own life work with renewed vitality. You dip into a source bigger than you—a great life, a book of wisdom, a resonant poem—and you approach your own decisions with added depth and breadth.

Night Work

Certain key turning points have structured my own life: leaving home at thirteen to enter a monastery, leaving the religious life at twenty-six, studying religion at Syracuse University and then teaching at another institution, being denied tenure and working privately as a psychotherapist, publishing a popular book and becoming a writer. Between being denied tenure at a university and becoming a full-time writer, I had a series of dreams all centered on a common image: a huge airliner trying to land on the crowded streets of a big city.

During these crucial years of my life, when chaos was the norm, these dreams kept my focus on the impact of external events on my soul. In life, I had to deal with many changes and challenges, and generally I was unsettled. I wasn't unhappy, but I had the chronic uneasy feeling that I had yet to find my place. I remember my mother once visiting me and looking around at my rented house. "Tom," she said, "when are you going to get your own furniture?" I was in my forties and I still didn't know what I was called to do for work. I could have gone in several directions, and I did.

During those several years the dreams of the airliner continued. I had been studying Jungian psychology intensely and took a sharp interest in my own dreams and those of the people I was counseling. I got to the point as a therapist where I didn't want a session to go by without consideration of a night dream. I found that even though the dreams were mysterious and never revealed fully or clearly what they were about, they offered insight that was invaluable. Just as inspiration empowers imagination, I found that night dreams reveal the very depth of the imagination in play as we shuffle along toward our life work.

As in the case of storytelling, I have a few simple rules about dealing with dreams: First, I follow James Hillman in his view that it is better to hold off on interpretation and let the images of the dream stir the imagination. It is more important to be affected by the images than to translate them into the world you know well. The dream could offer fresh insights, if it is allowed to stimulate ideas and not pushed into conclusions and resolutions that are already in place. My goal in talking about a night dream is to become more familiar with the depths, with the unknown and mysterious themes and motifs at work in a life.

Second, I can usually begin to make out some sense if I notice what the dreamer is doing in the dream. Often he will be defending himself or doing something that other figures in the dream don't approve of. I take these actions to be defenses against the rest of the dream. This pattern will not be found in every dream, but it is frequent enough to look for in every case.

Third, I suggest looking for a defining image or motif for the dream. My dream of the airliner appears to be such a deep, structuring image. I don't know exactly what it means, but I have some thoughts.

After having this dream image several times, I began to think of it as describing my condition of trying to "land" my ideals and ambitions in a real job. I was deep in the chaos and feeling every bit of its uncertainty and fragility. I had a boyish hope that everything would turn out, but I had no practical sense of how that might happen. I had huge ambitions and big promise but no suitable place to "land" them.

Then, at a rather late age, around fifty, things began to happen. I was married for the second time and became a stepfather, and in that same year I had a daughter. A book sold well and for the first time in my life I had some money to buy a house and raise a family. I finally had my own furniture. The landing field was being prepared.

I had to take my writing more seriously than before, and I got involved in marketing and public speaking, all of which matured me and made me feel that I had more of a place on the planet. At this time, I remember a dream in which the huge plane, which I knew well from many previous dreams, actually landed safely, if clumsily, on a busy city street, skyscrapers looming on each side and people lining the streets watching me.

My dreams of the airliner gradually stopped. But I still think of those dreams and feel that they helped me settle down and delve deeply into my life work. They reminded me that I had to make a clear intention to be part of the world instead of drifting up and away from it, that I was gradually learning how to land.

Dreams do not offer instant enlightenment, but they do lower the focus of the imagination and give it needed depth and mystery. If the imagination is too rational, it can't accomplish all that it is capable of. Noticing night dreams allows you to live in a middle place between ordinary life and your own depth. You can also better understand all aspects of the imagination, from art to conversation, if you are acquainted with the images and activities of the night dream.

People sometimes ask, if you are not interested in making useful interpretations of night dreams, then why bother with them? Interpretation isn't the only effective way of dealing with dreams. Recording them in a diary or notebook and talking about them with family and friends over time gets you acquainted with imagery as such. You will then notice the same imagery that you know from your night dreams in novels, poetry, and the stories you tell or hear about ordinary life. Noting your dreams in a serious way prepares you for the entire realm of imagery that holds the mysteries of your existence. You can go to an art museum and find echoes of your dreams in the paintings and sculptures you see. Understanding something about the art will help you appreciate your dreams, and, vice versa, being acquainted with your dreams, you will find it easier to understand the art. Both will expose you to the mysteries you live every day in your relationships and in your work.

Dreams are especially important in the process of finding your life work because you have to go very deep to reach it. Surface ideas and opinions are not adequate for dealing with something as profound as your life work. Dreams will give you hints about the dynamics of your search and about the nature of your calling. They will take you within range and give you hints about where to look and how to find it.

Nicholas of Cusa's descriptive words for chaos—Possibility, Being-Able-to-Develop, Underlying—all make sense in relation to this rather chaotic phase of the search for work. The time of chaos can be a painful period, but when worked closely with an active imagination, it can also reveal underlying possibilities waiting to be developed.

Sometimes what throws us as we try to find our way is not chaos but order. While it's true that many people can't find a direction for all the confusion around them and inside them, others are deeply unhappy because their lives make so much sense on the outside. Inwardly, they may be profoundly unhappy with a successful career or a high-paying job and feel stuck in their success or unable to change for financial reasons or because of their reputations. Many flounder in confusion, while others, we will see in the next chapter, feel imprisoned in the tower of their success.

CHAPTER SIX

LIFE IN A TOWER

Empty and be full;
Wear out and be new;
Have little and gain;
Have much and be confused.

TAO TE CHING

In a fairy tale a pregnant woman has a desperate yearning for rampion—a root vegetable used in salads, something like a radish—but there is none to be found. So her husband steals some from the garden of a sorceress—bad decision. The sorceress catches him and forces him to make a deal: He gets the rampion if she gets the child, in due time, who is to be born.

Time runs its course and the child is born—Rapunzel. Her name comes from the plant so darkly connected to her birth. Then the girl turns twelve and the sorceress demands that she be paid her due. She takes the young beauty and shuts her up at the top of a tower. But she takes care of the girl, climbing up every day on the long hair the girl tosses over the side of the tower, after chanting a song many children know by heart: "Rapunzel, Rapunzel, let down your hair."

One day a prince passes by and hears the girl singing. He is enchanted by it and watches how the sorceress chants her little mantra and climbs up the long tresses. Then when the sorceress is gone, he recites the magic words and climbs into the tower.

The two fall in love and begin seeing each other regularly. But one day the girl lets it slip that the prince has been visiting her. Or, in another version of the story, she notices that her clothes don't fit her anymore around the middle. The sorceress sees what is happening and cuts off her hair and holds it over the side of the tower the next time the prince comes. Seeing the sorceress, instead of the girl, the prince falls and loses his sight.

Rapunzel goes off to a deserted place and has twins, while the prince wanders around looking for her. Finally he finds her, and her tears of joy splash on his eyes, restoring his sight. They live happily ever after.

Like mythology and religious teaching stories, fairy tales reveal some of the patterns that offer challenges to human beings as they try to make a success of their lives. Fairy tales tend to be dark and full of malevolent figures who stand in the way of a happy outcome, just as life has its hazards and obstacles.

For some, the alchemy of finding a life work doesn't begin in chaos but in success. Several of my clients unhappy with their jobs actually worked in a tower, in a skyscraper or tall building, which gave them the illusion of success. They were not happy people, but they took pride in the perks of their jobs.

The story of Rapunzel speaks to the problem of finding your life work, when your problem is your own success. It begins with a woman's craving for roots—rampion. It's a strong metaphor: The woman seeks depth and rootedness, but she can't find it. So her husband tries to steal it from a witch, obviously a dangerous plan.

If you take the vegetable as the treasure of the tale, you see that the story is about the need for depth. The tower is just the opposite—the prison in which we find ourselves when we are cut off from our roots, the deep things that nourish us. This tower of wealth, prestige, or advancement can act like an enchantment, numbing us, making us forget the important things and keeping us cut off from real living—in the fairy tale, having a spouse, a family, and a home.

Many people find themselves successful and well-off at the top of the ladder, and yet they still feel unsettled, incomplete, and yearning for something more. They may look higher for signs of further progress, when they might better look deeper. Family, home, friends, and deep-seated spirituality might be the root nourishment they crave.

An articulate, educated, sensitive man, Brian, wrote me about his search for meaningful work. He majored in English and Latin in college, not thinking at all about the practical need to support himself and make a living. He decided to become a high school teacher. The whole process of being certified was "overblown," he says. "The principals were pompous, and my state certificate proclaimed that I possessed 'good moral character,' based solely on the fact that I acquired all the credit hours to become certified." He sounds like Sting trying to become a public servant.

With his strength in Latin, he tried to teach students who mocked and taunted him. He thinks he did a fine job, but his heart was somewhere else. By accident he stumbled into corporate training, where he was great as a teacher but knew nothing about his subject, which he says was over his head.

"I always felt disconnected from my work," he wrote in a letter to me. "I didn't choose to go into corporate training. Corporate training chose me. It wasn't an authentic experience with meaning or bliss. But again, I was good at it. People would not even guess that I struggle with this issue." This is an important point: People who look happy with their success, high in the towers of their achievement, may be painfully dissatisfied with their work. They find it difficult to express their unhappiness to those close to them because to all appearances they *should* be happy. They may feel that they have no right to complain.

Brian went on chafing in jobs that deep down he didn't want. He had to make a living somehow. He says he always feels like an outsider in the work environment. He hasn't yet found his place and he always craves something more. "I want a job where I am so engaged, and my work is intrinsically so meaningful, that there is no question that my work has value."

Here is man who has lofty, indeed spiritual, thoughts about work and what he would like to do, and has a good job in the corporate world, but he knows that some important ingredient is missing. He is searching for a deep connection. He is locked in the towers of the corporation and higher education. He is struggling with the Rapunzel problem.

I notice in Brian's words that he feels helpless. Though he succeeds at one level, and people see him as thriving at work, inside himself he feels disengaged, and the loss of that deep connection in his work is very painful to him. He is getting some of the benefits he wants from a job, but not the things that matter most to him—meaning, values, and a good fit with his nature. He seems to be the victim of circumstances and not in charge of his life.

I wonder if this personal issue, which surely has roots in his background, is the deep, underlying cause of his distress. Like Scottie, he keeps going after the right job, but there is no indication that he has taken a hard, deep look at himself. I suspect he needs a long inventory of his deep feelings and his past, because that is where his depth is located. If you keep looking for the job that will satisfy but fail to look deep enough into yourself, you may search for years without reaching your goal.

In the fairy tale the pregnant mother feels a strong need for rampion, but her husband steals it from a person with considerable power. There is indeed a tendency to plagiarize the depth of understanding we need. We borrow someone else's idea or latch onto a system or group. But we need our own depth of vision, not someone else's or some off-the-rack approach. We need our own history behind us, our own deep feelings, and our own root vision. A life work is different from a career in that it is always unique. No one has exactly the same calling that you have. You can't steal or borrow someone else's life work.

My job as a therapist would be easier if I had a dictionary of dreams and a user's manual for life's challenges, but each person presents a unique background and a particular style of being. My neighbor Tom doesn't have a mere father complex; he has a particular person for a father, someone who in turn had a particular person for his father. Although we might all like some simple answers, you have to dig into the unique complexity of your life to find the roots of your desires and anxieties.

The Rapunzel story also suggests that you may have to lose what is most precious to get the depth of nourishment you need. The story contains a quid pro quo: The woman gets her roots but loses her daughter. In Jungian approaches to fairy tales, the daughter would be a soul figure, representing the mysterious underground self that shows itself in disguised ways. We may get something of the depth we need, but we lose part of ourselves, specifically in a tower. When we reach high, we risk losing our depth.

While some people enjoy being above it all in their tower offices and cubicles, others feel uncomfortable in the rarefied atmosphere at the top. The successful executive may discover that his opus isn't over, once he gets the corner office. He still feels an emptiness that he wants to fill. He may think that his desire is about further success, while what his heart wants lies deeper. He may find the missing depth in his marriage, his family, or in avocations or social involvement and service, in a place where he can satisfy his need to make a more meaningful contribution.

In the story of Rapunzel there is much up-and-down movement, all by the grace of her long, beautiful hair. In human life it's also necessary to have open access between the height of our ambitions and the depth of our hearts. We need to move in both directions: moving upward on a scale of success and achievement, and moving downward, staying in touch with the past and deep feelings and important relationships. Highly aware people speak of "growing," and they look for an expansion of their life and vision. Rarely do you hear about "deepening," and yet this is an equally important process in which you become a more complex, more engaged person.

Scottie is usually stuck in one of the concrete solutions he has found, yet another unsuitable job, while in the depths he yearns for some unknown fulfillment. Brian is in love with beauty and ethereal intelligence, while he feels mired in jobs that take care of his family's material needs. You can sense a split in these two men between the quest for a good job and the need for meaning, connection, and identity. By *identity* I mean feeling that the job expresses who you are and fulfills your essential needs as a person.

If there is any single saving action in the fairy tale, it is Rapunzel's singing in the tower and the prince's ability to hear her voice. If we can still sing our hearts out in our towers, one day a prince might come, and we might recover that most precious of all things, the ordinary life. People sometimes spend years holding their unhappiness within them. They don't know how to express their dissatisfaction, or they don't feel entitled to complain. One day they discover that they don't have to be clear about their feelings. All they have to do is utter them in some way, like singing a song—literally or metaphorically. They have to let their unhappiness blurt out of them and be heard.

This is yet another sense of calling, the invitation to keep returning to your basic identity and emotions, especially when you get caught up in the rush of a career or corporate ladder. The higher you go, the more you risk losing touch with the ground of your background and deepest feelings. You can be disconnected from your past and your family roots, and you sense the disconnection as a feeling of emptiness or lack. You may be so preoccupied with the details of the job that you forget how important home and family and friends are to your greater life work.

Reuniting with Your Depths

A man once called up on a radio call-in show I was doing. He told the story of his move from Alabama to Wisconsin for a better job. He liked the place and the people, but at first there was something disturbing to him about his move. He became depressed and couldn't focus on his work. After a few weeks, wondering if he should move back home, he realized that he missed southern cooking. So he sent back home a request for grits and spices and recipes. He began making his own kind of food there in Wisconsin, where, he said, all they eat is cheese, and his depression lifted.

Depth may entail very concrete issues: personal history, deep feeling, cultural roots, and family traditions. These important considerations sometimes go untended in relation to work because we think that other concerns, such as success, advancement, increasing salary, prestige, and ideals, are primary. In this man's case, getting some familiar food was the key to getting back into his work with enthusiasm.

I remember a similar situation with a woman, Rebecca, who entered therapy complaining that she couldn't find the right work. She was moving from one position to another and couldn't settle down. She hoped to have a good marriage and have a family, but her dream seemed far from being realized. She was a very sharp, capable woman, used to being a leader and getting things done.

One day, in the midst of a conversation about a dream, the issue of food came up. Unusual for her, she began to rhapsodize about the great Jewish food she grew up with and how long it had been since she had tasted those great flavors. I asked her why she didn't make that kind of food, and she said that she didn't have time to do any elaborate cooking, and, anyway, her mother knew all the recipes and she and her mother rarely saw each other.

I suggested that she contact her mother just for the recipes and take some time out to cook. She found it easier to talk with her mother about food than more "personal" issues, and, in fact, her mother was pleased to have her daughter turn to her for this kind of help. They got along quite well over the food, and before long their relationship improved.

It sounds like a fairy tale, but eventually this woman shifted to an entirely different kind of career, met someone with whom she could have a real relationship, and had children. I have always felt that Jewish food was the solution for her out of a desperate career crisis. Of course, once she got married and had children, a whole new alchemy began, with its own challenges and ups and downs.

Connecting with your depths can be concrete and simple. You can revisit the places where you grew up or family members you haven't seen in a long while. Taking in the familiar sights from a different vantage point and listening to stories of times gone by can stir the heart and begin the process of reengagement with the depths.

Many people find themselves cut off from the culture in which they grew up. They may always feel like outsiders, a feeling that can be deeply unsettling and interfere with a career. They may suffer the status of not belonging just to get the rewards that the new life offers, but they may never sense that they are at home.

People might tell you to adjust and assimilate, leave your past and keep your sights on your new adopted society. It may be that you have moved from one country or region or city to another. There may be a language problem, certainly cultural differences. In some places, just moving across town involves some culture shock.

Here again the best solution might be to do several things at once. You can learn about your new world and even become more knowledgeable about it than the natives. You can certainly adopt the ways and linguistic habits of your new society and make an effort to fit in. At the same time, you can also nurture your roots, keeping in touch with friends and relatives and maintaining rituals of celebration and food. It's all a matter of realizing how important the deep emotions and memories are for grounding and supporting your more spirited adventures in the world. Your advancing career may depend on how rich your home life is and how loyal you are to your past.

We are back to the rampion and roots. The business of finding and maintaining a career may well keep you in the metaphoric tower, high and away from your grounding in family and culture. You may be misled into thinking that all your energy should go into the active pursuit of the career, whereas your work also needs the nourishing and supportive roots of your background. And the cultivation of that "ground of being" has to be concrete, not just wishful and not only intellectual.

Depth of Feeling

To feel something strongly is not the same as to feel it deeply. You may be so angry that you can hardly stay on the job, but you may be ignorant of the base of that anger. Or your anger may be a venting of dissatisfaction. Venting feels good at the moment, but it usually accomplishes nothing and may be destructive. And it has to be repeated because of its ineffectiveness. By venting anger, you can lose a job and harm important relationships. Fortunately, there are alternatives to venting.

If you reflect on your anger, you may realize that the present situation is not the cause of the full extent of your feeling. You may have encountered injustice before and bring your past anger over to the present, compounding it and making it difficult to deal with. You may find its roots far back in your life, maybe in your family, and possibly in your culture. You may be angry at white people, black people, Jewish people, Italians, Asians, the Irish, Catholics, police officers, tax accountants, or librarians. You can be angry at any group and carry that anger into your current life. These prejudices and bigotries need reflection. They can be dealt with.

Another source of chronic anger that affects work is a habit of always feeling victimized or at least submitting excessively to authority. Every interaction involves some exchange of power. Usually the power issues are slight and relatively equal. But at work there are many structures that put you under someone's thumb, and over time anger due to submission to authority can build up.

To get to the root of this kind of problem, which is widespread, you have to examine yourself and notice what your habit is: Are you the submissive type or do you enjoy having power over others? Within a moderate range, these tendencies don't cause trouble, but they are rarely moderate. Some people submit too readily and too much, and others enjoy their power too readily and excessively.

Both tendencies have roots, and if you can explore your emotional history you will see indications going far back of how these habits of relationship came into being. Again, reflection and self-discovery can modify them. If you can't deal with them alone, then you are a perfect candidate for some good counseling or therapy.

The intense competition in business and at the workplace gives rise to strong emotions that may be ignored, covered up, or reframed to look good. Recent studies show a great deal of hidden revenge and envy in businesses and also CEOs getting back at one another for firings and dirty dealings. The climate at work can be full of dark emotions that are not allowed to surface by name. Instead, an illusory atmosphere of peace and harmony prevails, while everyone knows about the true underlay of negativity.

This emotional intensity, dark and hidden, not only has a bad effect on business, it also confuses and discourages employees who are trying to establish careers and find their life work. Brian remarks that educational circles tend to be pompous, perhaps because of their lofty goals. He felt manipulated by an institution dedicated to knowledge and yet insensitive to the needs of people called to be educators. They used big words and ideas but didn't follow through with sincere actions. Again, language is contorted to cover up the real issues and make it difficult to deal with real emotions.

When Millard Drexler was pushed out of his CEO position at Gap Inc., he created a new company, Madewell, that sells high-quality jeans, sweaters, and accessories at a lower price. He said he wasn't motivated by revenge but that his "anger helps fuel my accomplishments now."[1] Revenge is a kind of anger that can be vented in tit-for-tat business deals that mirror political violence justified as retaliation. But we know from politics that that kind of revenge helps no one and ends up being tragic. Both anger and revenge can be converted into strong creative actions that are for the most part constructive. Drexler was accused of retaliation, but maybe what he says in his defense is accurate. His creativity was fueled by his anger.

If you are looking for your life work and carry deep, hidden anger with you, it will only work against you unless you submit it to an alchemy by which its constructive powers are released. Anger can become determination, personal power, a sharp mind, effective personal presence, clear decisions, and grounded creativity. Anger can be either very destructive or immensely useful.

I sense in both my friend Scottie and in Brian some anger that isn't fully grasped, owned, and used for good. It is still in the ineffective complaining stage, a form that is not very productive. All those complaints could be re-formed into personal strength, the anger indeed fueling accomplishment and creating personal effectiveness. Most people would benefit, in the pursuit of their life work, from the conversion of their raw anger into effective personal qualities of firmness, direction, and judgment.

Historians of religion use an unusual word to describe gods and spirits of the earth—chthonic. Among the chthonic gods is Mars, god of anger and war, who was also honored as the spirit nature's fertility and force. Rampion is also chthonic, a vegetable that grows in the earth, and represents the deep and difficult emotions.

A person might be called chthonic when she is earthy in language and style, when she allows her anger to operate effectively in her life and lets her hidden self be manifested. The goddess Persephone, the Underworld queen, was sometimes honored as an earth or chthonic goddess. In that underground role she was fearsome, deadly, and yet beneficent. It is sometimes said that fairy tales are later versions of mythology. We could imagine Persephone in the figure of the sorceress in the tale of Rapunzel, a spirit that guards both the underground fruit (Persephone's pomegranate) and the young woman (Persephone was a mere teenager when she became queen).

There is a form of creativity that reaches for the stars and is sunny and bright, but there is another kind, just as fruitful, that is dark and deep, more hidden than visible, motivated sometimes by anger and envy. This deep source of the creative spirit is difficult to express in our world because we have difficulty appreciating the positive qualities of the dark emotions. But they give a person depth, strength of character, and an earthy honesty and counter any tendency toward the sentimental and the naive.

First Aid for Tower People

Many tower people—owners, managers, CEOs—are happy at work because they know how to take care of their souls. They spend time with their families, their children, and their pets, and they may even go on a retreat regularly to take stock of themselves. But others show their shallowness in the superficiality of their tastes, values, and interests and in more serious symptoms of alcoholism, depression, and passive-aggressive behavior with their employees.

How does an ordinary successful person acquire depth of character? Some do it through tragedy, misfortune, or illness. Suddenly they discover what is really important in their lives. Some have a mysterious awakening. Suddenly they realize that their lives have been worthless, and they decide to turn everything upside down. But if someone interested in gaining some depth in his life wanted a strategy, what could he do?

Depth of character comes from admitting to yourself your complexity. If you are ambitious in your field of work, you can acknowledge this quality to yourself and those close to you. Shallowness can taint people's lives when they try to create a persona that hides their intentions and emotions. There is always a shadow side to work—money, sexuality, insensitivity, a need to dominate. When a person acknowledges these qualities, they are less destructive than if they are hidden, and they darken and deepen the face we show the world.

A deeper perspective on life may also come from appreciating the mysteries that surround you. Love, anger, competition, greed—these are emotions that come and go in all of us to some degree, and they are mysterious. Where do they come from? What do they want from us? You can reflect on these experiences and have substantial conversations about them with trusted friends. Often conversation remains superficial, but you can take it deeper easily by raising complex and challenging issues of emotion, values, and meaning.

Frequent attention to night dreams also creates a habit of reflecting on deeper issues. I was playing tennis with a friend, when out of the blue he said, "I had a dream about my wife last night. She was very sick and wasted away. I didn't know what to do, and I felt that life was collapsing around me." Now, this friend had never mentioned a dream to me before, and there, on the tennis court, it came out. I didn't know what to think of the dream: Was it about his wife? His own life? But we could talk about it briefly. I felt that a new level of friendship came with the telling of the dream, and we discussed it several times on other occasions.

Dreams convey some of the mystery of daily life, and the arts, too, similar in many ways to dreams, can give the pleasure that beauty offers and also raise serious issues. My wife is a serious artist and often does "public art"—artistic images presented in a public way, usually engaging the community in the making of them. Once, in a small New Hampshire town, she led high school students in a project in which several of them sketched their bodies in yoga poses on a blank wall on the main street. Then they filled in the outlines of their interesting shapes with a mud-and-clay mixture. They meditated before and after their work and engaged curious townspeople passing by.

People seeing those large clay images in meditative poses on the wall of a very small, quiet town were intrigued and filled with questions about the images and the young people doing the art. Can art be a serious way of life? Does it make a substantive contribution to society? Are these young people doing public art at an early age being prepared for a career, or merely a pastime? Public art can help people see the role of art in society and its place as part of a life work.

Other forms of deepening are inspired by traditional religious practices that don't have to be done in formal religious ways. Retreat, for instance, is a way monks deepen their already thoughtful lives. But I know many people in all kinds of professions who take time out, usually once a year, for reflection. They may go into nature or to a monastic retreat house or ashram or simply stay home for a few days and find renewal in simple withdrawal from the fast pace of life.

Corporations sometimes arrange "retreats" for their workers. The retreats I have participated in were valuable for taking people away from the workplace for a while to get to know one another better and to have conversations about the business. But these retreats often miss opportunities for deepening. They could include opportunities for silence or at least some quiet, for reflective live music and even art projects, and for discussion about the more personal and meaningful aspects of the company's activities and the workplace. The retreat could also include some presentations by capable leaders in psychology and spirituality.

Life deepens when you become more sophisticated about dealing with emotions and relationships. Many think that this part of life is purely natural and can remain unconscious and automatic. But we all need an education in these areas, which are always subtle and complex. I remember that when I first became a psychotherapist I thought I had good training behind me and plenty of study and reading. What I quickly discovered was that I had to learn to do this work by facing my own emotions, my past, and my relationships. I felt this special kind of learning more as an initiation through mistakes and painful discoveries than the learning of ideas. What I learned in doing therapy I applied to my own life, and then I turned the lessons around and applied them in my work. I suspect that everyone has to deepen the emotional life this way—through self-confrontation.

You can deepen as a person also by remaining close to your past, either your personal past or cultural history. The past offers many lessons in how to deal with life's challenges and how not to deal with them. In studying the past, you are considering your present and deepening your sense of who you are and where you live. Visiting historical places can stir your emotions and imagination, and that stirring is an important aspect of deepening. It shows that you are moving out of one stage of awareness into another.

All of these methods of deepening are effective if you have the imagination for it. You have to value living from a deeper center and enjoy the benefits of deeper pleasures and deeper relationships. Deepening has to be a value, something you want and appreciate.

In connection with our main theme, finding your life work, these ways of deepening can help you tap into your resources. A life work is not the same as a good job or a long career. It may not arise out of outward success. A life work is the emergence of your unique self, worked through and manifested in the things that you do. If you don't dig deep enough into yourself and see the world around you perceptively, your life work may always appear elusive. But if you live from a deep place, your life work will blossom like a flower.

We have seen two very different problems in finding a life work: floundering in confusion and feeling stuck in success. In either case, what is needed is serious attention to the development of one's character and the cultivation of a soulful life. The mess of an unformed life has to be brought into livable shape, and the hard heartlessness of external success needs a soul. For centuries, writers have said that one of the most important tasks everyone has to face is the care of their soul, the making of a personality, a life, and a society in which the values of soul—beauty, intimacy, creativity, and individuality—can flourish. The next chapter will show you how to continue in this quest.

CHAPTER SEVEN

CARE OF THE SOUL
AT WORK

Work is a kind of voyage toward self-improvement.

LOUISE BOURGEOIS

A woman in her twenties, Marianne, came to me once for help with her life. It's not quite right to say that *she* came, because her aunt, who cared for her deeply, brought her. Marianne looked terrible. Her skin looked bloodless and pale. Her eyes were red and watery. She hardly spoke, and then only in a whisper. She kept scratching at her arms nervously as she spoke.

Since she was almost silent and didn't want to be consulting me in the first place, it was not going to be an easy thing to help her. But I entered the situation with some hope. In the beginning I simply affirmed what she was going through and let her know that I appreciated her complaints. Over a period of a few weeks she began to relax.

She was in a very bad marriage and wanted to get out of it but had no way to make a living. She didn't know what she wanted to do with her life and couldn't imagine doing anything, given her extreme depression. Still, I encouraged her to tell her stories—of her parents, her past, her marriage, and her dreams.

One day she mentioned medicine. She admitted that she had always secretly wanted to become a doctor. But she was too old now, she believed, to begin the long and difficult training. She was in her late twenties. I saw a gleam in her eye for the first time at the mention of medicine, and I resolved to explore the idea, wherever it went.

The problems in her past were related to her religious upbringing, which was strict enough in her family but even more so in the church community, where, as a child, she was subjected to emotional and physical abuse. Her husband came from that church group and tended to dominate and control her.

Eventually, after more than a year of our conversations, in which she began to think positively about her future, she left her husband and entered medical school. With a scholarship, based on her brilliance in college, and financial support from her aunt, she managed the four years of basic medical education and then residency. During those years, she also took good care of her health and became interested in her home, her friends, and even her clothes. She woke up to her own life. Still, it wasn't easy for her at first to contemplate long years of study. But today she is a bright medical researcher, loving her work and thriving with a new husband and children. Now it's difficult to imagine the state she was in when she first arrived at my door.

A life work sometimes appears only as a glimmer in a dark mist of trouble. You have to focus on it, trust it, and let it take you into your future. People often look for large and weighty solutions to their problems, when the answer might take the form of a small beam of light. A therapist is trained to notice those slight shades of promise, but anyone can learn not to let them go by unnoticed and unheeded.

Marianne's is one of those remarkable stories that stands out from the rest. Most people make more gradual progress toward a life work. Marianne taught me how important it is, in moments of despair when life problems press heavily, to care for your soul. Slowly she began to make the necessary changes in life, allowing herself her dreams, taking care of her home and her physical well-being, and finally seeing the possibility of a new and exciting work life.

Marianne was in formal psychotherapy, but what she did with her life could be called care of the soul. The word *psychotherapy*, when translated directly from the Greek, actually means "care of the soul." (*Theraps* means "nurse" or "caretaker" and *psyche* means "soul.") In this sense of the word, a little psychotherapy on the more personal aspects of your life may bring your search for a life work to a point of revelation.

Marianne did not change overnight. Slowly and gradually she released herself from a bad marriage and unhealthy influences. Only then could she focus on her life, shaping and designing it the way she wanted it to be. She began with small steps—spending time with friends who supported her instead of criticizing and trying to convert her to their values. She liked folk music, and so she went with girlfriends to clubs and cafés she enjoyed. She avoided relationships with men for a while—she wanted to tend her own life and re-create herself.

One of Marianne's greatest challenges was religion. She had been brought up in a small-town church, and its teachings had lodged deep in her. But as she examined her life and became determined to make it better, she realized that she could remain devoted to her religion without being limited to the particular church where she grew up. With considerable emotional difficulty she left that church and began reading books that gave her support as a woman and as a responsible person. She enjoyed the process of reframing her spiritual life.

I refer to Marianne as a model of caring for the soul because she did such a radical job of it. She truly reinvented herself. Of course, her basic personality remained in place, and she continues to work through elements in her past, but she came through it as a new person. The change was a shock to many of her friends and family members. For most of them, it was a good shock, though some were scandalized.

Although caring for the soul is not as focused as therapy and counseling, it requires steady work. You give yourself to the unfolding of your opus, and you take steps to make life rich, clear, and satisfying. You diagnose what is going wrong, and you come up with concrete changes that allow your spirit to shine and your soul to settle into its own space, which includes finding work that satisfies.

When the issue of work presses, it is tempting to stay focused on matters of job and career, but it would also help to get the whole of life in order, or at least tend relationships and emotions and any concrete issues in daily life that are causing trouble. Your "psychotherapy" may be formal or informal, professional or just personal, but it can help clear the way for your calling to be manifested.

Becoming Your Own Person

A life work is a creative act. You assert yourself in a world that might well resist your efforts. You don't have to be pushy or aggressive, but you do have to be true to yourself, and that loyalty often requires assertion. But to be able to insist on your vision in the first place, you have to be somebody. You have to cultivate your own ideas and your style of working. As you go about on your adventure looking for the right work, you also have to tend your personal life in all its aspects—home, family, relationships, avocations, and service. The more substantial your life and personality, the more weight and strength you will bring to a job search or a career.

A good number of the people who write me for counsel complain of being pushed around, taken advantage of, and given lowly positions. They cite fellow workers or bosses who treat them badly. In these situations I see victimization and powerlessness, signs of at least a mild form of sadomasochism. I could tell these people to be stronger, but their efforts would probably be ineffective. You can't manufacture personal strength out of thin air. It would be better in the long run for them to cultivate the whole of their lives and simply become more substantial people living more substantial lives. Then they would have real heft behind them when they went looking for a job or went to work.

We saw at the very beginning that reflecting on the past is a good first step in the opus of the soul: You clear out obstacles to seeing your future. The next phase might be a focused effort to care for your soul, and here the past returns in a different way. You revisit the past now, not to find the roots of your unhappiness, but to be ready as a person to take on your calling. You are looking for identity, strength, and culture.

Many people find new vitality and direction toward a life work by rediscovering their cultural roots. Once, after returning from Italy, I saw an old friend who came from an Italian family. "Is it a good place?" she asked me doubtfully. I had just seen some of the best art the world has to offer, overwhelmingly beautiful displays of nature, and people who love life and are intelligent, welcoming, and lively. I gave her my enthusiastic reviews of her fatherland, and a year later she visited Italy herself. She came back with new appreciation for her roots and, I believe, went about her search for a life work with fresh confidence.

In your time of chaos, you may have been burdened by your past and by the people who made life difficult. But as the alchemy progresses you can work harder at all the material of the past, sorting it out and gaining insight. Gradually you gain distance on those painful experiences and they interfere less. You individuate. You become a separate person. You are no longer a copy of your family's values. You have friends and lovers, but you don't lose yourself in those relationships. You find your calling and your identity.

Dealing with the past is basically a two-part process: You own up to your experience, telling your stories as openly and fully as possible, and then move on, free of its dominance, into a future that you create. You don't deny the past or try to be completely free of it, but neither are you so preoccupied with it that you fail to make a new life for yourself.

Once in a while Marianne still asks me for an hour of consultation so she can deal with remnants of her personal history that still bother her. She sifts through her dreams and stories for insights. There is always more raw material to be sorted out and used for the present and future. But now the work is less urgent.

One of Marianne's central themes is passivity and aggression. She came to me feeling completely controlled by her family, her community, and her husband. Her aunt was an important exception. For Marianne to make such fundamental changes in her life required a fundamental shift in that power equation. She had to find, through her frustration and determination, the strength to build a new life in spite of all the heavy pressure around her to remain docile.

Being a unique person requires strength. You have to put yourself forward in a move that some people might interpret as offensively aggressive. I noticed this remarkably in Marianne: She came to me as a passive mouse of a person, but over time a deep strength in her emerged. Eventually, she showed herself to be a person of extraordinary passion and power. All that positive aggression must have been suppressed in her earlier years and hidden at the time I met her.

Personal power and passivity work like a teeter-totter: When they are extreme, they are far apart. One minute you display your strength, usually effectively, and the next minute you are the victim of some emotional assault. When they are brought closer to each other, power becomes personal effectiveness and creativity. Passivity turns into an appropriate and useful vulnerability. The two then are like yin and yang, enfolding into each other and coloring each other. Your weakness gains some force, and your strength acquires some flexibility.

Most of the people I know who are having trouble finding their life work are somewhat passive in style. They wait for something good to happen to them rather than make strong positive moves. The aggression comes later in the form of complaint, but then it is no longer effective.

Aggression need not go to the extremes of violence or manipulation. It can be a graceful, constructive way of getting things done. The simple act of making yourself known on the job or in a business is mildly aggressive. Showing your personality and presenting your ideas are aggressive acts, if they are done positively and not meekly. Finding your life work requires force on your part and that strength in turn depends on self-confidence and loyalty to your vision.

In the beginning of the search for a life work you delve into the past to find the elements that drag you down and those that might give you fresh ideas. Now, well into the adventure, you look for some kind of fulfillment of your past. You bring the parts of your life together, a legitimate goal in psychotherapy, and live a less fragmented life.

A Soulful Lifestyle

The personal, informal psychotherapy I am recommending in the quest for a life work entails creating a soulful style of living. That means living from a deep place and taking the time to tend your family, your home, and your friendships. It means being a real person on the job and being connected to the work you do.

Psychotherapy as care of the soul doesn't mean being introspective all the time, but it does require that you do your work and take care of your home life thoughtfully and with an eye toward individual choice rather than unconscious going with the crowd.

A soulful life is one of thoughtfulness, care, and engagement—you are present in everything you do, not just going through the motions. You give attention to the things that matter most. You take care of your body and your health. You make your home a place of comfort, welcome, and beauty. You educate yourself throughout your life in values and solid ideas. Your leisure time relaxes you, gives you a rich social life, and provides fun and play. Your spirituality is deep as well as visionary, and you incorporate contemplation, discussion, ritual, and prayer into everyday life, and you do all of this in a style that suits you as an individual.

From the matrix of a rich and thoughtful life, your life work emerges over time and you find ways to make it practical and workable. If you have a soulful life and home, you probably will not enjoy or tolerate a soulless workplace. You will want your career to match your sense of self—your values, your hopes, your style, and your deep needs. By *style* I mean the manner in which you do things, your own way of seeing things, getting things done, and designing your life.

I see cultivating a rich and thoughtful life as an extended form of therapy, or care of the soul. With this kind of care-ful existence, you don't just deal with crises and emergencies when they arise; you are grounded and reflective from the start. Your work life has a context and is fed by how you arrange your life elsewhere. Your work is thus consistent with who you are and what you believe. It expresses your private self, which is not then separate from your working self.

Getting your life less fragmented and yet richly multifaceted helps you make good decisions about work and career and the demand to make good choices continues throughout a working life. If you feel fragmented, you won't have the grounding and confidence needed to make decisions and guide your work as it proceeds. You may nervously wonder what to do next, if you feel torn in many directions. But if you are comfortable with the various dimensions of your life and have allowed them to mature, you will be ready to make the decisions that keep your life work dynamic.

My neighbor Tom has made a beautiful home, cultivates friendships, is active in his community, and takes care of his dogs. He is an adventurous person, and so these activities are not superficial. They represent a cultivated life, and he is able to take risks in his career because of the rich and stable home life he has created. Living with animals, by the way, can add to the soulful life by limiting your activities—dogs have to be walked and fed every day—thus giving you the graceful natural rhythm that animals enjoy.

The cultivated life I am suggesting is not predictable and dull; it is a civilized way of life. Civility can become superficial, but it can also serve basic human needs. Being friendly and helpful to your neighbors goes a long way toward living without anxiety—you get their support and companionship. Your city or town becomes a place you love and where you feel attached. Attachment is a great virtue in the life of the soul.

A civilized lifestyle rises out of an appreciation for gesture, language, and a positive worldview. The alternative is a detached, anxious, and hyper-busy lifestyle that only causes distress and problems. Civility can run deep, and you can cultivate it in a serious, consistent manner, giving it substance and letting it give your experience warmth and comfort.

People sometimes imagine their life work as a series of trials and tests, as a heroic task of slaying dragons and dealing with monsters. So it is easy for them to feel overwhelmed and discouraged. The cultivation of civility is medicine for such negativity: It generates a positive and constructive attitude and allows us to use our ingenuity to solve problems rather than blame others for them and curse life for its challenges. Civility offers an overall feeling of calm, enough at least to face problems from a positive foundation.

One doesn't want to sentimentalize the civil life. There is space there for anger and aggressive, critical activity. Civility requires self-possession, personal strength, and a degree of empathy, achievements that lie far beyond the usual unconsciousness in a society. Civility is rooted in a love of life, respect for people, and a willingness to go out of the way to be constructive and positive.

My friend Scottie is too angry to be civil. He sees himself in a battle against a society that doesn't care about him. What he doesn't see is that he doesn't show that he cares for it. He waits for society to change, whereas there might be some movement in his situation if he could change and become more civil. Society won't give him a job, he thinks, but if he were more open to society he might see better where he might fit in. He might catch a glimpse of a life work.

A Calling to Golf

One area where many people give themselves care and attention is sports. Play and recreation are as important to the soul as to the body, and many games have more mysteries baked into them than most people realize. Even spectator sports play an important role in helping the observer sort out his own emotions and memories of winning and losing.

With their astounding gifts of talent and physical assets, professional athletes clearly have a calling to sports. But most people enjoy sports as part of life. They may be passionate about golf, tennis, or swimming and dismiss them as mere exercise or play, but sports can be an integral part of your life work.

Sports are highly symbolic and usually ritualistic. You play with definite boundaries of time and space—a golfer knows the pain of hitting a ball out of bounds, and a basketball player knows the pressure of the clock. You may wear a special uniform and use the language associated with the sport. The rules are usually long and complicated. The ritual aspects of sports take them deep into the psyche, where we crave repetition and challenge.

The history of sports shows that in their distant origins the deeper meaning of the games was more apparent. For example, billiards was a game of "hazards" played on a green table to represent the green earth or the field on which life plays out. Golf has "hazards" and is played on a field of green. Sports are games of life. In our games we live out symbolically the challenges, defeats, and successes that are part of the bigger play of life, and therefore sports are important at a deep level.

Among other things, sports show that effort can be pleasurable. We also understand that the courage required on the football field or the gymnastics floor is real courage and is an important model for people witnessing the sport. Some sport is spectacle, showing us how to live and especially how to deal with challenge and adversity.

It is a short step from the sports stadium to the church or temple, insofar as sports involve ritual and contemplation—we watch games with intense absorption. In some societies the line was erased between sport and religion, as a priest might preside at the games. Like religion, sports are separated from ordinary work both in time and place, and we build our arenas and gymnasiums not just for practical purposes but also to keep sports separate from daily life. They are separate in the way religion is separate: designed more for ritual than for literal productivity.

Both attending sporting events and engaging in athletics are part of your life work and deserve attention and care. When you play golf, you are not just having fun or exercising your body, you are giving your soul many things it needs: ritual challenge, social interaction, exposure to nature, and sheer play. What you observe and learn on the course you can bring to the workplace and whittle down the barriers that fragment your life.

Companies that offer their workers opportunities to play sports together are responding to a deep need connected to the development of a life work. They are tying together the pieces of life, offering a way to contemplate and practice basic human virtues, and building community by extending the ways in which workers interact. Business and sports can be a useful combination.

Like anything else, of course, sports can lose their soul qualities and become empty. A focus on money, the need to win, extravagant costs—these extremes can chase the soul out of sports and render them useless for deepening the work life. But sports themselves are an important resource for connecting the development of personal excellence with success at work.

For the most part, care of the soul takes place within the intimate environs of your life: home, family, neighborhood, region. There is a larger dimension to this important activity, but in relation to the discovery of a life work it is mainly close to home. You deal with your relationships, your emotions, and your spiritual life. You create the conditions in which your work life can thrive. You take care of any fragmentation, unfinished struggles, and emotional preoccupations that might interfere with your work. You create a positive, somewhat tranquil setting out of which you can work powerfully and effectively in a challenging world.

CHAPTER EIGHT

BE GROUNDED, FLY HIGH

I've always said that I could write before I could read.

WOODY ALLEN

Icarus was one of those young boys who likes to get off the ground and fly through the air. One day he got it into his head to fly as high as the sun, and so he asked his uncle, the master craftsman and toy maker Daedalus, to make him wonderful wings for the job. Daedalus did indeed make a pair of graceful wings of wax, beautifully contoured and quite large, but he warned his nephew not to fly too close to the sun or the wings would melt.

Naturally, the young man, full of spirit and ambition, gave no thought to the limits his uncle warned him about. He soared and reached for the sky and came too close to the warm rays of the sun. The wings began to melt and down came Icarus crashing to the ground.

Some people get caught up in the Icarus syndrome at one point in their lives; others are perpetually like him—full of desire, somewhat reckless, and lost in their ideals. Often, too, they crash into a depression or some failed project and become disillusioned. Then they oscillate between grand ideas and failed experiments.

The Icarus person is filled with air. He becomes inflated with his grand ideas and has difficulty living in the real world, where challenges and realistic considerations discourage him. Jung referred to this figure of the psyche or spirit in a person as the *puer aeternus,* the Eternal Youth. Any man or woman might be dominated, at least for a while, by an excess of spirit—too much wind in their sails, too much glory in their eyes.

On the positive side, the spirit of Eternal Youth may give rise to idealism, inventiveness, enthusiasm, and a strong urge to be creative. On the negative side, it is often unrealistic and wishful. At its core there often sits a smoldering narcissism—excessive self-regard, extreme self-consciousness, and a bloated self-image. When this youthful spirit dominates a personality, many people deride it for its lack of responsibility. In relationships, the Eternal Youth is notorious for not being able to "commit." He can't hold a job and rarely realizes his ideals. He thinks up one project after another and rarely completes any of them. He battles time and is good at getting jobs started but not at finishing them.

A writer of this type may have a box full of half-begun projects or a list of great ideas that will never be brought to fruition. An athlete may be capable of great plays but unable to withstand practice. The computer expert can spend hours at a keyboard but only minutes taking care of children or cleaning his home. A person with this kind of personality lives at a quick tempo and doesn't enjoy long-drawn-out commitments. He likes speed, whether in a car or a computer.

I don't mean to be only negative about this *puer* spirit. Out of all the visionary hopes and dreams may come brilliant ideas. The lives of inventors and artists are full of the struggle to get their novel ideas grounded in real life. A youthful spirit keeps you young and flexible. It may also be the basis of a fervent spirituality; you see many people of this type in spiritual communities, monasteries, and ashrams. There, the *puer* spirit transforms into highly sensitive values and a dedicated lifestyle.

Many years ago I advised a graduate student, Ben, who later became a good friend. He was Icarus personified. He was full of fresh ideas and strong ambitions, and the academic institution simply felt annoyed at his resistance to fit snugly into its plan. He came up with what I thought was an excellent idea for a master's thesis, on the root meaning of philosophy, but the university refused to support either me or him.

Eventually Ben got his master's degree, and then, a surprise to me, he went to law school. He did well and practiced law for a while, but Icarus was still testing his wings, and Ben felt constrained in the law. He struggled for a while and then left his practice and became a sailing instructor on Lake Michigan. He continued his interests in philosophy and depth psychology and wrote very effectively about aspects of the law that people usually neglect. Since becoming a sailing master, he was written several fine books and completed important projects in depth psychology.

Ben has always had the *puer* spirit shining through in his face and eyes—it can make a person attractive, interesting, and exciting, as it did Ben. It got him into trouble at times, as when he couldn't get his good idea for a master's thesis approved and when he struggled with being a lawyer. But over time he found effective ways to ground his spirit without losing it: Teaching sailing gives him a challenging down-to-earth job, which is nevertheless suited to his personality—sailing is a classic *puer* activity, moving along fast driven by the winds.

Ben shows well how to connect the *puer* spirit to real life. He enters a solid institution—the university, law, and business—and takes from it what he can, and then he creates his own lifestyle, that of a writer and sailing instructor, that is successful and satisfying. The *puer* spirit doesn't need to be forced into reality; it can adapt to real-world situations. It can make an otherwise boring job exciting and help a person see possibilities that a more earthy imagination can't perceive.

When the spirit of the mythic boy inhabits a person, he may not tolerate the constraints of an elaborate work structure and may rebel against authority. But it can also help him adapt and transform work into versions that are congenial. Ben benefited from his stint in the law, but now he enjoys his work on the Great Lakes teaching people to be like him, a sailor, someone who lives by the changing winds.

Fame and Recognition

A craving for fame may be part of the *puer* syndrome, a focus on pose and image rather than the work itself. I once stood in line at a checkout counter in a supermarket. Directly in front of me was a rather minor national television personality. The checkout clerk noticed him and immediately began to melt with excitement. She stared at him while she packed all the wrong foods in various bags. Her expression was one you might expect to see on someone who had taken a large dose of Valium. In her delirium her eyes were wet, her lips Jell-O-like, and her neck stretched out in histrionic ecstasy. She looked at me and nodded vigorously at the star, hoping I would notice him and go into a paroxysm as well.

The craving for fame is the *puer* version of the more accessible goal of achieving recognition for the work you do. Most work is a two-sided business: You make something or offer a service, and your audience or customer uses and appreciates it. This is a useful pattern that helps keep society running smoothly.

There is nothing wrong with the desire for recognition, but in the best of scenarios it is the other side of performance. You do something well, and you are recognized for it. Yet if you do nothing, you still crave recognition. Often, the people who are so stunned by celebrity have not had the opportunity to feel ordinary recognition for what they do, and they imagine that appreciation requires the extremes of fame.

You don't have to do anything extraordinary to have the need for recognition satisfied. You can be great at selling shoes, making a hot dog, or installing a dishwasher. Someone will appreciate what you do, and tell you. That satisfaction may be part of the reason you go to work every day, because we all have an instinctual need for recognition and appreciation. We all need to be told, "Thank you. I appreciate what you have done. You did a great job." Recognition fuels the creative and productive life. It isn't an extra; it's essential.

The converse side of this law of interactions is the opportunity for you to offer words of appreciation when they are warranted. They are not a formality; nor are they meaningless. They may help the person serving you spend long hours at the job and put up with complaints and criticisms. I would recommend lavish appreciation when it is warranted at all, because our need is so great.

Deep beneath the fascination with fame lies a need in the human being for the superhuman, and ultimately the supernatural. We need a connection to that which is greater than us. Celebrities pump air into our imagination of what human life can be—the wealth, the opportunities, and the lavish lives we see celebrities enjoying.

But this fascination is also due in part to the difficulty we have today in feeling our own importance. There are so many people vying for jobs, so many jobs underpaid and undervalued, and so many corporations so vast as to be beyond human scale. Anyone would feel small in such a world. And so we crave a bigger life.

A young student once told me a dream in which he was in a hot-air balloon traveling slowly over a bucolic landscape. He could see people below watching him and wondering at the beauty of his aircraft. He was happy to be so high and yet visible in the brightly colored balloon. But then he began to ascend out of control. He rose higher and higher. The people below became dots on the landscape. He struggled to breathe and woke up in a sweat.

This is the dream of a portion of society, people who have high hopes for their work. But their dreams evaporate from their sheer emptiness. Dreams of fame and fortune may keep some people motivated, but others fly so high in them that they are far removed from real life. Somehow we have to learn to do both things: fly high in our ambitions and yet remain grounded in the practical world around us.

Saturn and Work

On the surface it may seem that work is work. Everyone knows what it is, and that's the end of it. But if you were to ask a dozen people about the nature of work, you would probably end up with a dozen different ideas. For one person, work is a way to make a living. For another, it's a productive activity. For still another, it's hard, painful labor.

These differences suggest that work is not just work. What it is depends on the way we imagine it and also on the way the society understands it. Our society largely conceives of work as strenuous effort, carried out under the watchful eyes of authority, for pay.

Work could be imagined differently. We could spend our hours at activities that we love to do. We could own the corporations in common. We could have lateral forms of management. We could reward imagination and creativity. Some organizations work this way today, but the majority do not. To do so, they might include the *puer* spirit as part of their deep myth, the way they understand and do things. There could be a place in the organization for the young man in the hot-air balloon who sees new worlds on the horizon.

Saturn is a Roman mythological figure who played a role in alchemy and astrology. He is often pictured as an old man, depressed, with his head in his hands. He is known to hoard money and be occupied with geometry and abstract structures. He is the spirit behind philosophy and theology. His metal is lead and his nature heavy. He likes rules and regulations and hierarchies.

Once, when I was teaching mythology and archetypal psychology to undergraduates, I asked them to go out and examine the university and come back and tell me which of the mythological figures it most reflected. They all said that it was Saturn. They found him in the university hierarchy, the many rules and authorities, the testing, the large and heavy traditional architecture, the organization of a classroom with the teacher at the head and the students lined in perfect rows of desks.

This is Saturn. We think people should work hard in spite of deprivations and pain. They should follow directions and authorities and traditions. They have to rise up through the hierarchy of command if they want to succeed. The corporations hold all the money and dispense it without undue generosity. We like people who struggle and make a financial success.

Mythology and alchemy recommend other alternatives or companion spirits for the Saturn workplace. I asked my students what a classroom would look like if Venus were the dominant spirit. They drew sketches of classrooms with plants and flowers, soft seating, good food, erotic art, and green walls. The Venus spirit has its own problems, but it offers considerable advantages and would certainly offset the Saturn element. A Venusian workplace would be a remarkable departure for most corporations and institutions.

During the Renaissance period in Europe, Venus was venerated as the spirit of beauty, grace, and pleasure. In Botticelli's famous painting *Primavera*, she presides over the Three Graces, at that time emblems of what were referred to as "the sweet life." At work, we could get at least a little of these Venusian qualities involved and perhaps humanize the environment and the activity.

Mythology presented Renaissance leaders with other possible images for work and culture. Mercury would emphasize style, mode of expression, a deep appreciation for the marketplace and commerce, and cleverness. Diana represented personal integrity, the virtues of the single life, and the love of wildlife and animals—and at work, solitude, focus, and attention to detail.

Our idea that work is "blood, sweat, and tears" is only one way of conceiving it. At the moment, Saturn reigns, but a free and flexible *puer* imagination might be able to introduce more convivial attitudes.

Youth, Age, and Sensuality in a Life Work

If you imagine your life work as a great burden, some Herculean task you must complete before you can feel that your life is justified, then maybe the Saturn side of the emotional equation has too much of an influence. You may have learned subliminally from the culture at large or from your family or from experiences on the job that work is painful, is something you don't want or like to do, and is a necessary evil. You may feel the weight of it and long to be liberated from it.

But imagine instead that a life work could be enjoyable. It may involve tasks that you would want to do whether you got paid or not. It could be more in the *puer* mode than Saturn. It could engage your ideals, satisfy at least some of your ambitions, and support your vision. In his book *The Soul of a New Machine,* Tracy Kidder described young men working at new computer designs. They were fired up about their work and labored long hours of their own choosing all because they were so enthusiastic about their work. He compared them to monks devoting their lives to labor they loved.

I have met pioneers in the computer business, older men now, who still have the flash of the *puer* in their eyes and feel a deep sense of accomplishment. They went into their work as believers wanting to take society into the future, and they didn't feel the drag of tradition and authority keeping them grounded in practicality and concerns about spending money.

You can perceive the *puer* spirit in the mission statement of the Tom's of Maine company, which reads in part: "To provide meaningful work, fair compensation, and a safe, healthy work environment that encourages openness, creativity, self-discipline, and growth."

These words are all *puer* language and are woven into a Saturn form known as a mission statement. A pure *puer* wouldn't bother coming up with a formal mission statement.

Ben & Jerry's ice cream company was also well known for its visionary approach to work. Its mission statement has a similar spirit though perhaps a bit more Saturn: "To make, distribute & sell the finest quality all natural ice cream & euphoric concoctions with a continued commitment to incorporating wholesome, natural ingredients and promoting business practices that respect the Earth and the Environment."

Now imagine writing up a mission statement for your life work. If you made it a combination of *puer* and Saturn it might be something like this: "I intend to find work that suits my talents and aspirations, while at the same time giving me enough money to raise my family with a moderate standard of living." A pure *puer* approach might be: "I want fame and fortune." A pure Saturn might say: "I want to do the work my family has always done—work hard, cover the necessities, and be satisfied with my state in life."

With all the vitality and spiritual vision he has to offer, the Eternal Youth is a powerful gift. He can keep you excited about your career, help you lift yourself out of untenable situations, and keep you going toward an inspiring goal. The downside is that when the *puer* is crushed by authority or disillusioned at the failure of a project, a heavy depression may follow. The boys of myth fly high and crash hard.

Saturn, too, has gifts to offer. He can give you personal weight and substance, help you lead others and create organizations, and use tradition well instead of always reinventing the wheel. It's important to feel solid in your job and manner of living, and this Saturn accomplishes without much effort. But he, too, can create problems such as rigidity, authoritarianism, and old-fashioned values and ideas.

I live in an area full of wooded hills where there is a company that clears forests and finds specialty woods to be used for fine building. The former owner, William, was a *puer* man: boyish in appearance, fun-loving, adventurous, and solicitous of his customers. One day he sold his company to a large corporation, and suddenly the tenor of the company changed. Its quality went down and its handling of people changed drastically. You could see then how William's spirit had shaped the company and infused it with a vitality that his customers appreciated. The *puer* spirit can be strong and effective, even in the context of an organization and in the midst of hard work.

It is possible for the boy of dreams to land his balloon and enjoy life on earth. Your task is to love his ambition and at the same time help him descend cautiously and gradually. You need not be afraid of him or embarrassed by him, even though he may take you into some follies and failures. You don't have to wait for him to grow up. But he has to come down to earth, fit in somewhat, and direct his creative urges toward productivity, community, and service, and then he will give you an identity and a life work.

Both the *puer* and Saturn may be more than personality types or styles of acting. They may be strong urges, largely unconscious, that drive a person in a certain direction. Some people can't help being ambitious and idealistic. They are possessed with such a spirit. Others couldn't be other than traditional if they tried—it is their "nature." For centuries writers have described these innate urges as the prodding of a powerful force called the "daimon." In the next chapter we look at the spirit that dominates us and moves us in certain directions toward a specific work.

CHAPTER NINE

THE DAIMON OF WORK

*I remember the day I saw my first exhibit of modern
paintings—my first Matisse and Gauguin, and, well, I had never
seen such glory. I realized then that I wasn't mad, not crazy, but I
had "ancestors" who had walked this way before me. It has to do, I
would say, with the explosion of a spirit and the defiance of tradition.*

MARTHA GRAHAM[1]

I have a friend, Judith Jackson, who has been captivated by
beauty and health all her life. At ten, she developed meningitis
and was cured, through her mother's intervention, at a spa. She
says she learned then that you heal best through cleansing the
body's systems and through careful eating.

Today Judith reaches around the world with her own aro-
matherapy beauty and health products and is currently directing
her attention to aging and health. She says that her career
began when she was in England having a massage with one of
Europe's leading aromatherapists, Micheline Arcier. "As I sat up after the treatment, I had a true epiphany. I knew I had found my
Calling. The treatment incorporated the philosophy of healing I

have always believed in: treat the whole person, mind, body, and spirit."

I have worked with Judith and so I know the depth of her involvement in her work and her commitment to her products, including teaching their use and marketing them around the world. If she lived in Renaissance Italy, people would have said that she was possessed by the daimon of beauty, perhaps by the spirit of Venus, goddess of beauty and sensuality.

For the ancient Greeks a daimon is an unnamed urge that pushes you in a certain direction. It is the force behind the passion and tenacity of your yearning. If you experience the daimon of love, your whole life might be centered on the quest for a perfect mate. If the daimon was beauty, you might, like Judith, pursue ways of caring for the body. There are also daimons of aggression, home, sport, and creativity—the possibilities are infinite.

The Romans believed that a child is born with his daimon, or in their language, genius. It's a fertile idea: that the deep passion and drivenness that stays with us all our lives is there from the beginning. It becomes more defined as we grow older, or perhaps we simply learn more about what it is and where it can take us. It can also wake you up with a startle, as it did Judith lying on the massage table, offering you a kernel of vision for your future. This is one of the functions of the daimon.

The daimon is a primal, creative urge. It doesn't inspire a single, well-defined career. When you step back and look at the many things you have done, you may see the root inspiration and an essential direction. Judith has gone from modeling to acting to the pleasure and care of the body. It may be difficult to pinpoint exactly what the common thread is in her life, until you recognize the work of the daimon of beauty.

Like Judith, you sense the daimon as a passion, an urge you

can't ignore, and a direction that you yourself might never have chosen. The appearance of the daimon is like an eruption or even an intrusion into your life. You may fight it, thinking that it is a negative influence. I have heard many dreams of clients in which a door is left ajar or a window opened a crack. The dreamer is afraid that an intruder will appear to threaten and do damage, but the intruder might be the creative daimon, who might well indeed upset the status quo.

Socrates said that he lived his life according to the dictates of his daimon. "The favor of the gods," said Socrates, "has given me a marvelous gift, which has never left me since my childhood. It is a voice which, when it makes itself heard, deters me from what I am about to do and never urges me on." Through sensations of inhibition it let him know when he was going wrong and through silence left him alone when he was on the right track. From Socrates, we can understand the daimon as the guidance offered by an inner wisdom, more an impulse than a thought. But it worked for Socrates because of his devotion to a daimonic life, a habit of listening to its urges and especially to warnings.

When I was teaching religion and psychology at Southern Methodist University, the golfer Payne Stewart was a student in two of my classes. He hadn't chosen a career yet. He came to me one day and asked me to help him decide whether to become a professional golfer or to go into business. I asked him to bring me a dream or two. I knew that his question couldn't be answered through rational analysis. We needed a deeper, more mysterious hint about his nature and his calling.

We discussed his dreams, and he got the sense from them that he should take a chance on his real passion, golf. His father taught golf and that close relationship played a role in our discussions and probably in his decision. Eventually, he went the way of his daimon rather than the way of safe reasoning. I felt that he already knew deep down what he wanted to do—the nature of his calling and the daimon that drove him—but he needed permission or encouragement to follow his impulse.

The Roman orator Cicero once said that it is the animus, another Latin word for daimon, that gives us our identity. The impulse toward golf defined Payne's life. He brought such style and personality to the game that you can't imagine him just going into business and playing golf on weekends. It's the same with anyone: You find out who you essentially are by allowing the daimonic power in you to shape your life.

In ancient practice, when people actually spoke of their daimon, they didn't always name it. Sometimes they thought of the classical deities as daimons—the daimonic Aphrodite, goddess of beauty and sexuality, or the daimon Demeter, mother earth. Usually they imagined the daimon as pointing in a certain direction while remaining nameless. As I said, Judith Jackson seems motivated by the daimon of physical health and beauty. Payne Stewart shaped his life by the dictates of the daimon of golf. From the beginning, I have been moved along by the daimon of spirituality, art, and healing.

To recognize your daimon, you have to ask yourself what mysterious power keeps you fascinated in a particular direction. You can see the daimon clearly in your friends: the one who usually provides the food at a social gathering or activity; the one who is always off traveling; the one who always has a book in her hands. It is more difficult, perhaps, to pinpoint the daimonic influence in yourself.

You can look back on your life, even if you are young, and notice the focus of your fascinations, interests, and desires. You may have obscured your daimon by trying too hard to be reasonable and conventional, so you may have to look beneath the surface. What compels you? Where do you typically lean?

You can always take the route of Socrates and notice the nature of your inhibitions. Do you hear a "voice" telling you not to do things? Not to take this job. Not to move to this city. Not to trust this company. If you are going to live daimonically, you take these inhibitions seriously. You decline a job simply because you hear a faint warning within. You trust your deepest intuitions. You remain alert for inner guidance.

To live by the dictates of your daimon requires a willingness to ease up on your rationality and your desire to control your life. You listen more and pay attention to signals from within, especially to inhibition and hesitancy. You consult yourself, heeding the daimonic force, which, over the years, you may have come to know. Sometimes the daimon appears as a strong intuition.

The trouble with intuitions that seem to tell you to back off is that they are difficult to distinguish from fear and simple hesitation. You may have to experiment many times with intuitions before you can more easily sort them out from anxiety. I have heard people say that they don't want to travel because they have an intuition that there may be trouble or an accident. But they can't tell if it is a true intuition or mere worry that they pick up from the latest news.

Living with the daimon means learning over time the particular ways it presents itself, so that you know better when to follow it and when to go your own way. Intuition is different from rational judgment: When you make a decision based on facts and research, if you're wrong you know that you made a mistake somewhere. With intuition, you may not be right all the time. You tolerate mistakes, but in return you get a more comfortable sense of what you should do and not do. The daimonic voice is deep-seated and is connected to your personality and destiny. You can learn to trust it without being naive or without giving up your healthy skepticism.

When you are trying to see your life calling, you pay attention to any sensations of being in the wrong place, even if by all external criteria you seem to be successful. That's the Socratic approach to the daimon. You can also notice deep desires that move in a different direction from your current work. Desire is not a bad thing. It lets you know what you need at a deep level.

But you don't have to act on desires just because they are there. It may take some experimenting and exploring before you know the full meaning of your desires. You might talk about them with friends and family, sorting them out in true alchemical fashion. You might look for connections between them and your night dreams. You might even prepare yourself to work closer to the area of your desire, while you continue at the job that gives you a living.

The Greek philosopher Heracleitus said that the daimon is your character. The urge to enter life in a particular way may be so much a part of you that it shapes your very identity. Your life work is a response to that inner directive that helps you make one decision after another as your career tacks along creating your life and shaping your personal qualities.

Judith is like other people I know who follow their daimons. When she has to make a career decision, she checks in with that impulse that has guided her all along. She asks herself, "Is this what I really want? Is this me?" All the facts and reasons may point in one direction, but if her inner impulse isn't in accord, she will decide differently. I have watched closely as a project of hers shifts many times until she feels it is right.

One way to follow your daimon is to keep the channels open

between your inner and outer life. Give even the slightest emotional reaction against your work some consideration. In the case of the daimon, you listen and then evaluate. Notice when you sense, without logic or clear expression, that the situation isn't right. Pay attention when your friends tell you that you're on the wrong track. They may not be right, but their opinions have to enter the vessel. Mistakes at work, a resistance to going to work, or lethargy may be signs of the daimon.

Some people choose to make a good living in a job or profession that pays well, and they satisfy the daimon outside of work. I had a friend many years ago, Victor, who was a dentist. He loved his profession, but he placed his real passion in music. He led a men's choir and wrote and arranged music for it. His social life was largely centered around music, and when he was directing the choir you could see his spirit soar. I felt the daimon in his willingness to spend hours of his free time working for the choir.

In Victor's case, he did not just have a hobby or avocation to fill out his work. He was driven to the music and seemed happiest and most at home when he was directing. Not being a professional musician, he knew his limitations but was able to do enough with his local choir to fulfill the demand in his soul.

People who live with the daimon don't follow the crowd. Over time the daimon fashions a unique person who isn't swayed by practicality or the common wisdom. Judith is clearly called in the direction of creating a product she loves, teaching people how to use it, and marketing it effectively. Each of these three facets of her work she accomplishes in her own style, and it appears to me that her individual style, so important for a sense of accomplishment, comes from her loyalty to an inner, indefinable taste and direction.

Style is the product of a strong calling. When you "follow your bliss," in the words of Joseph Campbell, you automatically develop a style, which is nothing more than the manner of a person who is sure of his place in life. Style gives pleasure, in particular the pleasure of being an individual in a sea of sames.

In his usual contrary way, Oscar Wilde once said, "In all unimportant matters, style, not sincerity, is the essential. In all important matters, style, not sincerity, is the essential." Style is the particular way in which you do things. It develops over time from your interaction with the daimonic influence at the core of your being. You become an individual, you develop character, and you live and work in a certain manner.

I notice that my neighbor Tom has a subtle but clear style in his language, his dress, and his comportment. I'm not surprised that he is uncomfortable in his current job in a large corporation, because institutions often try to erase style from their employees. Style suggests individuality, which may be perceived, erroneously, as a threat to the institution. Many people equate the smooth running of a business with conformity.

I glimpse Tom's daimon partly in the direction his fulfilling career has gone—working with people in an organization dealing with finance—and partly in his developing concern for the future of his town. His daimon seems to be taking him away from the work that has defined him successfully for years, toward a more independent cause, a utopian idea of a humane community.

The daimon is a power, not just an idea. That's why it's not quite right to refer to it as "inner wisdom." As a power, it tends to urge a person away from the safe and secure life into areas of risk. It's easier to see the daimon at work in an inventor, say, who startles the world with a new idea, than in a person humming along in a steady, unchanging job. Yet it could be that the daimon has been heeded and at least for a while allows some tranquillity and security.

Tom's sheer individuality embodies Heracleitus's idea that the daimon generates character. His willingness to leave a corporation that has the resources to keep him financially comfortable for a long time suggests that he is following a different kind of guidance. He is determined to seek his own destiny, and that conviction is a sure sign of a daimon.

Scottie, on the other hand, seems disconnected from a daimonic passion that would give him a path to follow. He feels lost. He has no passion for a particular work and feels that he could go in almost any direction. This absence of a daimonic urge leaves him vacant and confused. Instead of speaking of his daimon, he has to deal with the demons.

Living with your daimon is a responsive kind of life. You constantly listen and consider the impulses and signs of its presence. You make sincere and concrete efforts to shape your life according to the daimon. You develop trust in its signals, even when the facts point in a different direction.

One of my own struggles has to do with my work as a writer. I admire artists who go their own way and develop their own quirky styles and individual modes of expression. One of my favorite writers is Samuel Beckett, who many people find incomprehensible and quirky to the extreme.

But, no matter how I try to be such an individualist in my writing, I know that I am driven in a different direction, toward helping people get along. I am a therapist on the page. I try to care for souls as I write about the soul. I feel slightly embarrassed about my writing, since it is so simple and helpful, compared to my dream of being a bizarre Beckett figure. My daimon is consistent, and as long as I follow it, my creative life generates enough success to give me pleasure.

Today people think that they should be reasonable and conventional in their approach to a career and proceed according to judgments from outside rather than urges from inside. They want concrete experiments with work and testing to guide them, because they don't trust the thrusts that come from inside. They also don't have the imagination to consider such an approach—where would they learn about daimonic forces and how to deal with them?

The Struggle with the Daimon

W. B. Yeats was another who lived according to his daimon, but he described it as an "antithetical self." He said that the daimon has a different point of view, compared to your own conscious and willful self. It wants you to go one way, while you are trying to make a life of a different kind. But out of this struggle comes a creative life.

Living with a daimon may not make you happy. There is something insane about the work of the daimon, in contrast to the rational approach to career that college counselors might advise. It may steer you toward an unexpected way of life, but in its own way it could help you fulfill your dreams. In ancient times the daimon was called a demiurge, a world maker, a creator of life.

Rollo May, the existentialist psychoanalyst, stressed the capacity of the daimon to possess and overwhelm. Your current life may be too small to contain or withstand the power of the daimon, or maybe you haven't opened up enough space in yourself, haven't become big enough a person to contain it. Even so, May treated the daimonic influence as a source of the creative life and the root of love.

The daimon often asks more of you than you think it does. You do what you think is right. You move in the direction you feel driven. Yet you may get caught in symptomatic behavior related to your daimon. If your daimonic focus is Dionysian—a need to break boundaries and limitations and live life with considerable abandon, you may drink too much. If your daimon is Aphrodite, you may lose yourself in a sexually undefined and complicated life. If your daimon is like that of D. H. Lawrence—to break society's molds and structures—you may have trouble keeping your important relationships intact. You may glimpse your daimon hiding in some addictive or maladjusted behavior, such as alcoholism or careless sexual encounters. These are passions, of course, but they may be outlets rather than inlets into your fate. They may distract you just at the point where you need focus.

My friend Scottie's alcoholism appears to be the heart of his problem. It gets in the way of keeping a good job and is destroying his marriage and family. Involvement in a twelve-step program has helped him, but he still wanders from time to time. And when I speak with him, I don't see the daimonic in him in any positive way. He feels flat, having no aspirations and no sense of direction. He has no fire in him to make something of his life. I suspect that his daimon is still trapped in the scotch and large quantities of wine he drinks.

Scottie's efforts so far to find the spark of his existence have been half measures. He hasn't confronted himself and come to grips with his origins and past experiences. He has done some foolish things, like making advances toward a babysitter, and he has only excused his behavior. He hasn't fully owned up to his wildness and so the daimonic remains buried and disguised. You can see its spark in his unwise actions, but you also see that it hasn't been accepted as a serious element.

The daimon provides the energy and direction a person needs to move into new areas of work, but it requires a creative and sensitive response. As Yeats says, you may have to wrestle with this force, engage it, and allow it a serious role in your life decisions.

In my own case, I am a fairly quiet and retiring person. Externally I would not appear to be a model for a daimon-directed worker. And yet, deep within, I feel the presence of something far beyond my will, taking me in certain directions and creating a life work for me. I can trace my interest in the soul fairly closely over the course of my life, and my interest in spirituality has clear roots. But how do I explain my career as a writer and the success of a few books that has brought me so much interesting and vital work in television, radio, medicine, and religion? I couldn't have planned all this. Yet neither have I been savagely driven in this direction. I feel that a constant and somewhat alien force has shaped my work life for many years.

I had a friend in Ireland, a man I consider the greatest Irish writer in recent times, John Moriarty. John writes like a man daimonically driven. He sings, repeats, chants, rhapsodizes, and prays on page after page of his books. Many readers find him difficult to read because of the range of his references to myth, literature, and philosophy. Shortly before he died, I visited him in a Dublin hospital where he was being treated for cancer, and I felt completely uplifted by the constancy of his particular kind of faith and his loyalty to the muse that inspired him on the page and in person.

His imagination is huge, and he tried teaching at universities for a period in his life, but eventually he abandoned that career because it didn't fit the vast extremes of his imagination. But he didn't leave that life easily.

"The night before I came back to Connemara I wept, because I knew my time on the high street, of being a young man engaged in a young man's pursuits, was over and I was reaching solitary confinement, insecurity.

"But like the seal coming up to the breathing hole I had to come up for air. I had to be myself. On a day when I felt I had no

soul I went to a river which would give soul to you. I flourished
again in a new way and I never forgot or regretted the leaving."

This is a life lived daimonically. It isn't without fear and anxiety, but it knows how to keep on track. Sometimes, as the ancient
Romans and Greeks knew, you can find your daimon in nature.
John knew that the river, an ancient image for life's flow and twists,
would restore him deeply to his own path.

Expect a Struggle

Anyone who has described the daimon as a creative force has emphasized the struggle that is part of it. In his last writings Jung
talked about his own life in this way. "I have had much trouble," he
wrote, "getting along with my ideas. There was a daimon in me. It
overpowered me. I have offended many people. I had no patience
with people—aside from my patients. I had to obey an inner law
which was imposed on me and left me no freedom of choice. A creative person has little power over his own life. He is not free. He is
captive and driven by his daimon."[2]

Jung's daimon led him into the deepest mysteries of human experience: séances, astrology, alchemy, UFOs, dreams, coincidences,
and religion. He is still ridiculed for the range of his concerns and
is dismissed as having been mentally unhinged, but this statement
offers his point of view. What for some is instability, for others is
loyalty to a daimon.

For all the struggle, Jung did not suffer emptiness in his work
life. Just the opposite; his daimon led him to a highly original and
satisfying life work. In spite of his rueful words at the end, he was
not an unhappy person. He comes across as a complicated man
who understood the mixture of forces and emotions that go into a

full life. That he was often ridiculed and dismissed as crazy and eccentric didn't seem to bother him, and he knew consciously that following his daimon would lead to a controversial life work.

Jung's critics tend to be those who envision a rational life as the norm and ideal. Jung never did such a thing. Theoretically he defined the self as a midpoint or overlap between the conscious and reasonable life on one side and the life of passion and unconsciousness on the other. Personally, he lived this multidimensional life and became an effective healer. People all over the world came to him for his guidance.

Jung's example gives us the opportunity here to note that a life work is not the result of rational planning and preparation alone. You have to develop attitudes and strategies for allowing the daimonic force to show itself and allow yourself to experiment with it. This results in a *complicated* life, using the word in a positive sense. You do things that to others might seem unreasonable, but you do them because you know they are necessary for the fulfillment of your destiny. You may not choose them for yourself, but you do them because you see their necessity.

Daimonic Education

At any age, you can allow yourself experimentation with some of your less than rational ideas. My father began piano lessons at age ninety-four. I know a banker who goes on retreat in Maine each summer to take courses in photography. Martin Sheen routinely shows up at rebellious and visionary events. These are not earthshaking activities, and yet they hint at a daimonic force that runs against conventional wisdom or at least stretches the notion of vocation.

Socrates, the model of life lived in relation to the daimon, also showed through his own example how to educate for a daimonic life. He never told his students what to think or do but rather drew out their own inherent knowledge. Time after time he asks questions that lead his students toward revelation and understanding. He isn't teaching his students how to think as much as how to be open to the interiority of the subject at hand. In this way, he prepares them to be attentive to their impulses and stirrings.

Accordingly, the Greeks conceived of education as *paedeia,* the development of mind, body, soul, and spirit into personal and social *arête. Arête* is often translated as "excellence," but it implies bravery, wit, and personal power. A person with *arête* is not just an outstandingly accomplished and learned person, but rather someone with special powers that rise above the human. *Arête* implies a daimonic way of life, where a person derives strength, mental keenness, and imagination from a source beyond his rational mind.

Modern education aims at the absorption of certain standard ideas in the arts and sciences and the attainment of skills for a particular job. An employer doesn't look for personal power and depth of perception as much as the ability to handle standard challenges. We no longer educate young people to be open to the daimonic force that would give them their life work. Instead, we tell them what work they should do and help them adapt to it.

Today, we have surrendered to a view of the human being as a mechanical being ruled by a brain, and we see education as instilling skills and facts with the purpose of having a successful career and making as much money as possible. We ignore the education of the heart and the revelation of a deep power and direction within the person. As the Greeks understood, society fails in such a condition. Not only the individual, but the community, too, needs the force of the daimonic to deal with the challenges life continually presents.

I knew a man in Dallas, Robert Trammel, who was a poet and thinker. I didn't know Robert well, but all my contacts with him were inspiring. As far as I could see, he cultivated the life of the outsider. He joined established organizations, but there he was always a gadfly offering alternative points of view. He created his own magazine for experimental writers and was always encouraging artists to be bold and show their work and go their own way.

Because Robert preferred to be an outsider, he may have looked like a wanderer who had never found his way. But if you were ever really within his scope, you knew that he had a strong, enviable sense of calling. He didn't have a typical job, but he had a clear vocation.

In a poem called "Dreaming" he wrote the following lines, which convey the spirit of this book and perhaps his own quirky life:

A life is mostly remembered in bursts of short stories
Beautifully interwoven with people, places, and events
A word, a picture, a smell can set it all in motion
And you can close your eyes and see it clearly
As if it happened only yesterday

I don't know if Robert would have spoken of destiny and the daimon, but he did appreciate the "bursts of short stories" that make us who we are. Even though we do go from episode to episode, life can have a purpose, which may be glimpsed, as Robert says, in a mere smell or word. *Purpose* and *destiny* are huge words, easily inflated and overblown. Still, they convey an important ingredient in a life work.

It was only when Robert died that I saw the purpose in his life and work. Suddenly all the little pieces—the small magazines, the short poems, the ill-attended readings, his comments from the back of the auditorium—they all amounted to a powerful life work, and I felt overwhelmed by the clear direction of his labor. Several times he invited me to join him in some of his small publishing labors, but I never had the time. Now, seeing the gem of purpose in his work, I regret my decisions.

Imagine if each man and woman were free to unleash the daimonic force within them in their life work. A family grocer can be full of daimonic power as he or she takes care of an entire neighborhood. A daimonic accountant would be a valuable asset to anyone trying to live with economic intelligence.

Citizens so educated and inspired would be a potent source of social advance. They would bring their unique passions and acquired intelligence to political decisions, instead of following the masses in mindless devotion to party politics. They would create real community, the thoughtful gathering of empowered individuals.

Daimon and Duende

Implied in the very idea of a life work is the element of individuality. Having your own life task, you can bring passion to your everyday experience. You unleash your desires and fears and loves and let them bring life to your work. You wouldn't picture a person doing his life work depressed and lethargic. You would see him engaged, opinionated, impatient, and strong.

Toward the end of his brief life, Federico García Lorca wrote a famous essay on what he called *duende*, which powerfully evokes an important element closely related to daimonic living. *Duende* is impossible to define, but it is the palpable passion you sense in an artist or athlete who reaches a point of superhuman power and produces magical effects with unexplainable skill.

Lorca, possessed of considerable *duende* himself, puts it this way: "There are neither maps nor exercises to help us find the duende. We only know that he burns the blood like a poultice of broken glass, that he exhausts, that he rejects all the sweet geometry we have learned, that he smashes styles, that he leans on human pain with no consolation."[3] He is the passion that rises up through the feet of an inspired guitar player.

Lorca himself connected *duende* to the daimon. "The duende I am talking about is the dark, shuddering descendant of the happy marble-and-salt demon of Socrates, whom he angrily scratched on the day Socrates swallowed the hemlock."[4]

Duende allows you to do your life work with a passion and brilliance that surpasses human skill. It is deep inspiration, and it applies to all kinds of work, not just to that of artists and athletes. In them we behold the magic of which we are capable in our own lives and professions.

Duende is the ability to put your life on the line for what you do and to do it without regard for the approval of polite society. You do it because you are compelled and filled with desire and willing to risk. You take chances and flirt with failure and risk going out into the world as an individual possessed with outrageous passion.

Perhaps one of the reasons people don't find their life work is that they are unwilling to be host to *duende*. Your life work may ask more of you than you wish to give. It may take you in directions you purposely have decided to avoid. It may even ask you for complete surrender and absolute risk.

The extraordinary genius I had for a teacher of music composition in my twenties, Donald Martin Jenni, had a calm but powerful daimon. It isn't surprising that a person so gifted in music and languages—"superhuman," other students said of him—would be led by a daimon and filled with *duende*. But Jenni was always understated in his manner, and he spent his life quietly teaching music at a university. In his case the role of educator allowed him to show the breadth of his genius and the depth of his knowledge. It offered him the right setting for his version of *duende*. Being just a composer or performer would not have given him the proper stage.

One of his students, David Lang, said in a eulogy: "Jenni loved music not for the career of it but because he loved thinking about it. . . . He was intensely quiet, restrained and private, generous and moral. I have to say that his quiet scared me at first, because I had trouble reading the subtlety of what emotional cues he gave out. But he was gentle and could be very funny, and he had a kind of glow about him when he spoke of something he believed in." Jenni's "glow" and his ability to "scare" a student with his quiet are both signs of the power that drove him in his life. The daimon that presses on a person may not be obvious and may not make for an explosive life; it may show itself in a quieter power and glow.

Another lesson about the daimon we can take from Jenni is the difficulty in pinpointing the nature of the work associated with the daimon. At first glance, it would appear that Jenni's daimon was musical, but then you have to account for the extraordinary talent in languages and his lifelong passion for monasticism—he spent time in a monastery in his retirement years.

I spent many hours in conversation with Jenni, studied his musical scores as he was writing them, and listened to him perform. He was my first experience of watching a true genius in action. When I first heard about daimon and *duende*, I felt I had encountered these two powers in a teacher who could be passionate and almost violently inspired without much display.

Lorca talks about the creative passion of *duende* being close to death. I take that to mean not just literal death but the death of your plans, your familiar identity, and your control. You let go, free-fall into the unknown, and allow something powerful to happen. How else can you obtain the power that is not in your full control?

As any artist or musician knows, you can't work with powerful effect if you can't let the daimonic force have plenty of influence. If you are just rational at your work, the result will feel only rational. Working from a deep place creates an impact that goes deep. But the same is true of all work and of making your life meaningful through what you do. You have to allow your deepest passions to show through.

But this doesn't happen by sheer will or at a moment's notice. You have to prepare all your life for work that has the flash of the daimon in it. You have to deal with resistance, fear, habit, and the wish to control. You have to learn what it feels like to be open to the daimon. You have to allow your personality to take shape in accord with the daimon. None of these achievements is easy or quick.

Of course, it's possible to be too open and unprotected, but even a modest welcome to inspiration and intuition might be just what you need to empower your life and give it meaning. A life work appears in many guises, and you have to be alert when it shows itself. It probably won't announce itself logically and formally, but only through hints and opportunities. You must take your intuitions seriously, following them through as far as you can and noticing also where you hesitate and feel blocked. The daimon guides both positively and negatively.

Ultimately daimon and *duende* stream together and you find that living from a deeper place gives you vitality. You don't have to push yourself into life because the daimon's urging is sufficient.

At a certain point in the Work, the alchemist would take special notice as the stuff in his retort changed to a reddish color. This phase he called *rubedo,* the reddening. It was the point where a feeling of vitality and power entered the picture—the red of passion, vitality, and aggression. Red is *duende.* A person is incomplete without it, and a life work is not fully revealed without its influence.

When you move closer to your life work, you might well experience the reddening of your being, your work, and your world. You come to life and feel engaged with what you are doing and with the people around you. You discover that when you are doing the right work, you are the right person. Your work makes you feel alive and gives you an identity. This is an important phase: not the end of the process, but a significant turning point.

Introducing daimon and *duende* into the equation, we see a life work as passionate, forceful, and dynamic. We are building up toward a vital sense of work, far beyond a mere job or career, but rather the sense that we have a job to do on this earth, that we have been called to make a contribution and to be a factor, no matter how small or unrecognized. We grow into a life work, becoming bigger in the process, bringing along our passions, energies, and expectations.

The daimon rushes you into your work with such passion that you more readily become deeply involved. Socrates said that his daimon was the power of love, and, indeed, a daimonic force can help you love what you do. It allows you to be less cautious, more abandoned, and more connected to your work, and it helps you open your heart and give your life to what you are doing.

CHAPTER TEN

LOVING WHAT YOU DO

The alchemists thought that the opus demanded not only laboratory work, the reading of books, meditation, and patience, but also love.

C. G. JUNG[1]

Brother Kieran was an Irish monk who lived in the heyday of Celtic monasticism. He was skilled in the elaborate calligraphy recognized the world over as one of monasticism's greatest achievements. There were two loves in Kieran's life: the experience of community and the labor of his art. He tried to keep both together, but at times one would triumph over the other. He would get involved with his brothers eating dinner or cleaning animal stalls and neglect his manuscripts, or he would spend the night with quill in hand by light of a candle and fall asleep in choir the next day.

It came to pass that the community was in danger of coming apart due to lack of funds. The monks desperately needed to find a source of money, and the abbot turned to Kieran. "Would you please work overtime on a manuscript that we can sell and stay afloat?" he said. Kieran was more than happy to devote more hours to his art, especially for the sake of the community.

He worked all day and far into the night, so focused on the swirling, colorful letters and tiny, deep-tinted images from monastic life that he was unaware of the time passing. He put his love into every turn of filigree and every intricate knotted background. Finally, he finished the work just as dawn was arriving at his small window and he went to the abbot's office to show it to him.

When he left his cubby in the scriptorium and entered the monastery, he was amazed to see a huge building full of monks cheerfully working in the kitchen, cleaning floors, and waxing the thick wood doors. In the abbot's office he encountered a man he didn't know but who spoke with authority. "And who are you?" the man asked. "I'm Kieran," the young monk answered. "Here is the work I was assigned." He showed the manuscript to the new abbot.

"Yes," said the abbot. "These things happen. We have all read the story of Brother Kieran, who disappeared one hundred years ago, of his skills and devotion to community. We have searched for decades for this manuscript, and now we have both it and its creator. Praised be God."

Most of us have moments when we are so involved in work we enjoy that the time goes by faster than seems possible. At other times we watch the clock and the minutes go by like hours. While you can't expect every job to be like that of Brother Kieran, is it too much to ask for a job that you can love?

We talk about looking for the right job or finding meaningful work, but what we really want is work that we can love. We face two challenges: to find work that we can love and to find love for what we do. These may be two paths to the same goal, but they are distinct.

One problem we have in discussing love and work is that we often have a sentimental notion of what love is. Do you have to be rapturous about your work to love it, or are there kinds of love that are less extravagant?

You may think that work has nothing to do with love. You have to make a living, care for your family, or just survive. But if we are pursuing a life work, not just a job, love is an inescapable issue. How can you have a life work if you don't love what you're doing?

Kinds of Love

The Greeks distinguished among several kinds of love: eros, agape, and philia. Eros is largely misunderstood today, since we have reduced its meaning to sexual love, especially of a dark and reproachable kind. Agape is the word used most often for love in the Gospels of the New Testament. Usually, though not always, it refers to compassion for your neighbor. Philia was much praised and discussed in ancient Greek times and again during the revival of Greek culture in the Renaissance. It is friendship, plain and simple. All three of these loves affect our work, and strangely, perhaps, the most important is eros.

The earliest appearance of eros comes with a particular branch of ancient Greek religion called Orphism, after Orpheus, the singer and charmer. In the Orphic creation story, all of existence began in Night, a primal goddess. With Wind she became pregnant and laid her silver egg in the lap of Darkness. From the egg came the child, Eros, also known as Phanes, or light. He was the god of love whose job it was to stir passion and inspire unions.

Early Greek philosophers applied this work of eros to the world at large. They saw him as a kind of creator, uniting the various opposites in the cosmos to form a coherent whole. Even in our small lives, eros has a creative aspect, and, in this older sense, to be erotic is to have a lust for life, wanting to shed light wherever possible and bring disparate things together.

Of course, this grand notion of eros is far from the modern notion of eros as shady sexual love. Yet the Greeks also told stories of how Eros was the son of Aphrodite, goddess of sexuality, and ran errands of love for her. So, we can't remove sexuality in some form from the erotic life.

Eros and Pleasure

You can apply this broader notion of eros to an ordinary work situation, especially those circumstances when you love your work either because it taps into your creativity or because it contributes so much to making the world in which you want to live. The peak moments of working offer a sense of vitality that few other things can match. These erotic rushes at work may be rare, but they can make a career and a job feel worthwhile.

When we say that you can love your work in an erotic way, it means that it can offer rewards that are sexual in an extended sense of the word: sensual delight, desire, pleasure, and connection. Keep your idea of eros big, and then picture your work as having some delight associated with it. Imagine that you could want to do the work so much that you can't wait to get to work, where you become deeply absorbed in your projects. This is all eros.

Eros also involves pleasure. In speaking with people about their work, I find that they rarely talk about pleasure. They are usually concerned about the basics of making a living and being successful. But when they are so focused on the practical or on the future, they may miss opportunities for pleasure, and pleasure is an important ingredient for keeping you attached to your work and making the required effort to get it done. If it seems odd to speak of work and pleasure in the same breath, that strangeness may be due to a tendency to associate work with pain.

We don't think of pleasure as a key element in work, and yet it may play a subtle role. You may be interviewing for a new job, discussing the duties of the position and its compensations, when you notice something about the architecture, decor, or landscaping that strikes you and has an impact. The pleasures that lure you may not be central to the job but incidental and largely unconscious, certainly not the focus of the interview.

Generally, we undervalue the simple pleasures that may be part of a career or position, and yet they play a significant role in job satisfaction. A corner office, a window, a nearby restaurant, an interesting neighborhood, a well-made desk—these are obviously not the central substance of a work life, and yet they can be of great importance. An executive once told me, "I can get up in the morning to get to work because of my friends here." A lawyer said, "What I like most about my job is the old building where we have our offices."

We can look at pleasure in work in terms of spirit and soul. The spirit enjoys reaching goals and arriving at peaks of success, and these spiritual pleasures are important. But the soul is fulfilled in momentary, ordinary, and more tangible experiences, such as the feeling of being at home or with family and experiencing beauty and pleasure. Accomplishing or producing something is important in work, but so is the pleasure of the process.

Enjoying work doesn't mean that you like every minute of it or that it is free of problems. It means that overall and deep down you take real pleasure from being in the workplace, using your tools, doing your job, and working alone or with others. The great philosopher of pleasure, Epicurus, from whom we get our word *epicurean,* said that some pleasures are passing and others are deep and lasting. You may not find passing pleasures in your work as often as you would like, but still you might enjoy the deeper pleasure of knowing that you are doing the right thing in the right place.

Pleasure is an aspect of that particular love called eros. If you can work toward loving your activity, your product, your coworkers, your workplace, and your customers, you would be making your work more erotic. The more eros in your work, that either you find in the work or bring to it, the more likely it will take you to that treasure we call a life work. In fact, as you move toward a life work, you may find the surest guidance in your need to love what you do.

This book is all about finding work that you can love, but you can also bring love to your work. If you are chronically angry or frustrated, those emotions will prevent you from loving your work. You can't separate your emotional life into partitions of work, home, social life, and personal psychology. If you don't love your work, consider dealing with your emotions in every aspect of life.

You can also create an environment favorable to love by cultivating a civil, friendly manner. Today people tend to adopt a pragmatic attitude and may automatically think of manners as superficial, but a conscious attempt to practice civility, maybe even to a greater degree than seems natural, can help the work environment and lead to a deeper kind of love.

Friends at Work

In the history of love and of the soul you will find friendship placed high, if not at the very top of values. Though it seems ordinary and simple, friendship is one of the most powerful forces on earth. It is a kind of love, a special brand, that can support you as you search for a life work.

Friendship is a relatively constant love not disturbed by the ups and downs of passion as much as romantic love is. You don't need a ceremony to initiate a friendship, as you do with marriage, because friendship grows slowly like a small garden rather than arriving in full bloom like a huge floral display.

Friendship is a broad category that sometimes means intimate connection and other times a loose tie. There are good friends, close friends, and friends who may be more like acquaintances—it's sometimes difficult to know which it is. However strong the connection, friendship allows you to go on in your life with companions who will support you and be with you and talk with you. These are simple but essential gifts.

All of these qualities of friendship affect your quest for a life work. Friends are there to respond to your choices. They care about you, but they are free to question and criticize.

One of the famous friendships affecting life work was the relationship between Sigmund Freud and C. G. Jung. The day they met they spent thirteen hours in intense conversation. They not only had much to talk about, but they liked each other and wanted to be in each other's presence. For years they wrote long letters to each other and remained friends even though other friends of each tried to interfere.

There were problems with the friendship from the beginning. Freud wanted Jung to inherit his role as leader of the psychoanalytic movement. Jung had his own ideas and questioned some of Freud's basic principles. Over time these differences became stronger and took on a tone of rancor. Jung was shocked to see how much, in his view at least, Freud expected conformity and filial submission. Freud was surprised at the independence Jung demanded.

After seven years they broke up their friendship. Freud began talking about Jung in disparaging terms, and Jung developed a distinct approach to psychoanalysis, complete with his own following. Here we see the complexity of friendship and the arc of its life. Although Jung broke from Freud, at the end of his life he admitted how important Freud's friendship had been to initiating his life work.

In all matters of love, we have to be careful of the tendencies to sentimentalize it and to require too much of it. A friendship may not be perfect and yet still be a crucial piece in the development of a life work. Marsilio Ficino, who wrote passionate letters and essays about friendship, said that you meet yourself in a friend. You discover a companion who is your mirror reflection, even though the friend might be very different from you.

One of my closest friends is a former professional football player. From the outside Pat and I would seem to have little in common. Physically he is a giant compared to me, and very athletic. Even in more intimate matters we are different: He appreciates the dark side of life in a tangible way, while I tend toward the positive. He is interested in the corruption, violence, and accidents that he sees around him. And yet at the core we are much alike, and the intensity of our conversations may have to do with the common take we have on events.

Neither of us likes conventional thinking. We are both liberal if not radical in our political slant. We both appreciate the magical and the mysterious in ordinary life. In his life, Pat is working out issues that are of great importance to me personally, and in our frequent letters I make advances in my own quest. I think I offer something similar to Pat.

Maybe Ficino is correct: In our friendships we encounter ourselves, and in our lovers we engage the other. Both are important, but for the discovery of our life work, seeing ourselves with another or in him allows us to know better who it is that is seeking his destiny.

Pat has helped me in my career because he knows so intimately what I am trying to do and who I am trying to be. Our differences keep him from merely supporting me and allow him to give me a perspective on my actions, but our commonality allows him to know my destiny even better than I do. In most of my books I acknowledge his influence, but it would be difficult to say concretely what that contribution is.

With a good friend or a group of friends you don't go out after your life work alone. They are extensions of yourself and you are an extension of them. You are followed, supported, accompanied, and sometimes led by them toward your destiny. You go out in love rather than mere mind and brawn. The love of friendship, philia, surrounds you like a halo bringing your heart into action and giving you at least a minimum of the quality Epicurus says is the most essential in all human endeavor—tranquillity. This is not passivity but a calmness of heart and freedom from anxiety. Friends don't take away all anxiety, of course, but they help deal with it, perhaps minimize it, and lead you to another essential kind of love—community.

The Communal Nature of the Self

I have another old friend, Mike, who is tall, athletic, handsome, and gifted. He has a big smile that reflects a big heart. But when I met Mike many years ago he seemed lost and rather obsessed. He didn't have a job and didn't seem to know what to do with his life. He was interested in the deep theological and philosophical questions. More than interested, he seemed compelled to pursue them with a focus that was intense. He wrote to famous authors asking them to help him with his quest for understanding.

Mike would go back and forth from being relaxed and having a good time to becoming focused on the questions that disturbed him. We swam and played tennis and became close friends. To this day we tease each other without mercy and then sit down to serious conversation.

Several years ago Mike was playing tennis at a fitness center when he noticed that members were tossing out their old athletic shoes in the garbage, and the shoes were not in bad shape. He got an idea. He began collecting used shoes, washing them and sorting them, and sending them to parts of the world where children especially were forced to go barefoot, thus exposing themselves to disease. Mike's simple idea turned into a major operation, and today he sends tens of thousands of shoes around the world. There is no telling how many children he has helped. He gets very small donations, enough to keep him and his teenage son going, and he still washes and sorts the shoes.

Mike's story is an example of the kind of love the Greeks called agape. It is not at all like romantic love, with its particular kinds of passion and focus on two individuals. It is not friendship, because Mike doesn't have any personal contact with the people he serves. And yet it is truly a form of love, unsentimental but very strongly felt. For Mike, this form of loving has saved him, given him meaning, and created a life-shaping work.

In the alchemy of becoming a person and finding your way, love is like the furnace, which, along with the glass vessels, is the most important instrument in the process. Love provides the heat, the energy by which the work gets started and is sustained. Mike's work with the shoes is not blissful at every moment. It has all the heaviness of drudgery and toil. Mike doesn't get much recognition, and he rarely sees the fruit of his hard work directly. Some days he gets discouraged.

A passion for social justice and a desire to make a difference keep Mike going at his excellent homemade work. That passion was in Mike long before he found a vehicle for it, and it all came to pass because of the nature of his concern, his awareness, and his desire to do something. This is agape, and it is a deep aspect of community.

Community is not a group of people or an organization. Community is an outlook toward life in which you define yourself in relation to the world around you rather than only in connection with yourself. It is the opposite of narcissism. It is what develops as your narcissism advances from self-love to love of the other.

Most formal approaches to the job and career search center on the individual. A counselor assesses the person's abilities and aptitudes and matches them with potential jobs. Or he might think about which kind of work will fulfill the individual. The focus is on the person.

Mike never sat down and asked what he should be or how he could best fulfill himself. He kept his eyes open and saw where there was need and suffering in the world, and out of that communal outlook he created a work. In him the notion of work as the process of becoming a person and as a way of making a living come together. Which came first is a question of the chicken and the egg.

Community is a matter of defining yourself in relation to others. Are you an isolated, self-absorbed individual, or are you a participant in society? Whether you can ever find your life work while wholly focused on yourself is a question worth much discussion. Even hermits and solitary artists can feel profoundly connected to the world in which they live and work. You don't literally have to be active in society to be part of a community, but if you are not cognizant of the society of which you are a part, then you risk being cut off, limited to your own concerns, and, of course, lonely.

As a therapist, I see many people absorbed with their emotions, their loss of meaning, and their failing relationships. They can't help but be concerned about their own lives. They are shocked sometimes when I suggest looking for a volunteer position or in some other way serving their community. Need is always within walking distance, and it wouldn't take long to find your niche in service to a needy world.

Becoming more involved in community helps resolve many personal emotional problems, which are often due to anxiety about the self. Rather than getting beyond the self, I recommend enlarging the sense of self. Your soul is a bigger and deeper conception of who you are, and it extends outward beyond your personal life to include your community and the cultural and natural worlds around you. For thousands of years people have talked about *anima mundi*, or the world soul, which is the tangible depth and vitality of the universe in which you live. Jung once said that the soul is not in you, you are in the soul. It is a powerful way of reimagining yourself to think of yourself as part of something larger, rather than to think of everything being inside you.

Community is not an arrangement of people; it is a form of love. It is felt, enjoyed, and enacted in service and celebration. If you can achieve agape, communal love, in your feeling and attitude, you are a long way toward finding your life work.

I speak of "community" rather than "your community," because the perimeters of your community shift and change. Your community might be the people at your workplace or in your corporation. They might be your neighbors or fellow citizens. Ultimately a full sense of community embraces the entire world, the people, creatures, and objects that are part of it. From that large vision, a large life work could emerge. You have only to stay close to your love, nurturing it and allowing it to intensify.

Part of the problem people have as they struggle with a career or even a personal emotional issue is their intense focus on themselves. This focus gets tedious and eventually deprived of vitality. We need other people in the scope of our concern to help forget about our obsessions and put our problems in context. Psychotherapy itself can aggravate this problem by increasing the isolation of the discussion, and so it's sometimes a good idea to offer service to the community as a form of therapy.

Loving Your Work

For most of his long life my uncle Tom worked the 125-acre family homestead in upstate New York. The farm had been settled by my family after they emigrated from Ireland in the late 1800s. My uncle loved being a farmer, loved every inch of the land, loved the animals, and loved his part of the world. But he was never sentimental. He got up early, worked hard and long, worried about his income, and never treated the animals as pets. I never heard him say that he loved the life of a farmer, because he didn't speak so directly. But it was clear from everything he said and did that he was passionate about every aspect of his demanding life. You could sense his love in the attention he gave to every fence nail, every closely honed cutting blade, and every bale of fresh-cut hay.

If you like the product or service you are involved in, enjoy the circumstances of your labor, and appreciate the people who work with you, you can safely say that you love your work. And that love makes all the difference. It allows you to be engaged and intimate with what you are doing. You are present to it, and your desire to do your work wakens the deepest part of you, your soul, and gives your work humanity and individuality.

Although my uncle the farmer was a giant in my eyes, he was not perfect. Every couple of months he would get stone drunk, and I felt then that my uncle had disappeared. I couldn't wait for him to return. I don't know the roots of his drinking. I heard tales that he was once so disappointed in love that he decided to live ever after as a bachelor and drowned his sadness. I'm sure that isn't the whole story.

You can love your work even if your life isn't in perfect order. Love doesn't demand perfection, but it does ask you to give yourself with less reserve than you would prefer. It asks for an openness to life—maybe just the ability to love a piece of land and to keep memories intact.

Anger and other negative emotions can interfere with the love of work. You may express your anger passive-aggressively, showing up late, not having projects done well or on time, or speaking badly about your company or your superiors. This misdirected anger stands as a block between you and your work, preventing love from forming.

You may harbor an old disappointment or yearn for a position that has never been available to you and therefore you can't focus on the job you have enough to love it. For a number of reasons your mind may be elsewhere than on the job, and not being fully present, you can't find any love for the work you are doing.

You can't force love into existence, but you can clear a space for love to arrive. Here alchemy enters the picture once again. So much of that work requires finding all the debris of a life, putting it in an effective vessel, sorting it out, and letting the resulting solution purify your heart. *Purificatio* was an important stage in the ancient process.

You put your old resentments, disappointments, failures, tarnished ideals, and competitive envies and jealousies into the pot and let them be sorted out. Just recognizing all this bad stuff for what it is, especially in the vessel of a friendship or therapy, gets the purifying action under way. The tendency is to pretend that you were innocent all along, whereas the alchemical process marks an end to naïveté and innocence. You don't cover up your dark emotions any longer but rather place them one by one into the container where you can see them for what they are, feel their unpleasantness, and then watch them change.

In old illustrations from alchemy, the material looks black and sludgy, but a white bird flies up and away from it—an image for the purifying taking place and a new innocence emerging. You can't love your work when you are cynical or holding grudges, but when you achieve the sophisticated innocence that comes from self-analysis, you are free to feel positive emotions once again. You have gone through a catharsis, a cleansing of your attitude that allows new life to stir.

My friend Scottie tells me about a new job, and he becomes enthusiastic as he describes the skill and personal qualities of two of his managers. I feel some hope for him, because I know that it takes a degree of innocence to appreciate a fellow worker, especially someone in charge. Previously, Scottie was cynical and could only talk badly of his superiors.

Now, if he can grow to love his work, he may finally be on the road to a renewed life. He doesn't have to think of this new job as the end point of his search, but bringing a purified attitude to it will make all the difference. He can move forward from there. Love is the heat, the energy, and the drive that can keep him in motion.

It's difficult to use the word *love* in relation to work without sounding sentimental. The beauty of alchemy is that it simply describes a process. It doesn't inflate the role of love, but it does express the importance of devotion to the Work. When it shows the Work turning red, it signifies not only a new level of vitality, the red of blood circulating once again, but also the red of the heart, the heat of love.

I developed my philosophy of work when I was living in a religious order. I was taught to include the menial jobs assigned to me—keeping records, cutting grass, and pruning trees—as essential to the life. I was encouraged to love work as a spiritual path.

CHAPTER ELEVEN

TO WORK IS TO PRAY

*When you do something, you should do it with your whole
body and mind. You should do it completely, like a good bonfire.
You should burn yourself completely.*

SHUNRYU SUZUKI[1]

The mullah Nasrudin once got a job as a porter at the Bazaar. One day he had to load bags of grain onto a cart. The foreman noticed he was carrying one bag while the other workers were each carrying two. The foreman asked Nasrudin, "Why are you only carrying one bag when everyone else is carrying two?" Nasrudin answered, "I'm not so lazy that I'd make only one trip when I can make two."

On the surface Sufi stories about Nasrudin, the trickster, holy man, and teacher, sound like simple jokes, but at a deeper level they offer a spiritual lesson. This story suggests that from a spiritual point of view work can have motives very different from simply getting the work done. Nasrudin lives by his own rules and both puzzles and worries the authorities. Is he trying to avoid heavy labor, or is he living outside the accepted norms of society? Since Sufi stories teach deep truths, is there some basic idea about work hidden in this thought-provoking story?

Jesus told a similar story about laborers in a field. Some arrived early in the morning, some in the middle of the day, and some in the late afternoon, and yet they all got paid the same wages. It doesn't seem to make sense. Some see the story as a metaphor for salvation, but recent scholarship suggests that it is about a radical shift in values, a shift that could well affect the way you work.

A Reversal of Values

Both the Nasrudin and Jesus stories have many implications, but let's focus on one of them: When you consider the spiritual aspects of work, you have to use a logic that is different from the world's reasoning. You may step outside issues of salary, hours, duties, and opportunities for advancement to consider ethics, meaning, and the social contribution of the work. While salary and related matters are important, it may ultimately give you deeper satisfaction to develop your spiritual vision at work.

You don't work only to get paid your hourly wage, nor do you have the same goals as everyone around you. A father or mother advising a child, "Don't take a job just for the money," is saying something similar. Don't worry about the math that ensures you exactly the right pay for your labor; consider other reasons for working. Step outside the logic that makes your labor a commodity.

If a human being is made up of body, soul, and spirit—a very ancient definition of a person—then we each have spiritual needs as well as physical and emotional ones. Spirituality affects our work in three key areas: It leads us to engage in work that gives life meaning; it calls on us to do work that is ethical and carried out in an ethical context; and it inspires us to do work that makes a contribution to society.

If you use these three criteria in choosing a life work, the possibilities quickly get narrowed and you are on your way toward a work that suits you. Certain jobs will be meaningful to you, but probably a great many more would feel meaningless. They might have meaning for another person, but you are unique. Meaning is an aspect of your particular spiritual outlook.

I have a friend and former client, Susie, who worked as an insurance agent when I first met her. She had hopes of creating her own business and making a good living in that field. But it didn't suit her, and she was not succeeding. She came to me depressed, and she saw no connection between her work and her low feelings.

Next, she got an exciting job managing a band. This was a step forward for her, and she found much more meaning in this work as compared to insurance. She spent several years doing the hard work of arranging jobs for bands and taking care of the many details of performances and money. I thought she had found her calling.

But Susie had always expressed a keen interest in psychology. When I first got to know her, I noticed how much she valued the work of psychotherapists, almost venerating their work. I lost touch with her for a few years, and then I happened to bump into her. She was then in training to become a therapist, and I had never seen her happier. "I've always liked my work, even some aspects of insurance, but I never felt that it was really meaningful, for me," she said.

Susie's crooked path is an example of how spiritual issues can help a person find the work of her life. Her desire to help people was evident in her various occupations, but it came to the foreground in her decision to become a therapist. In training, she felt somewhat embarrassed being older than her fellow students and suddenly making very little money. But that foolishness is part of the story.

One key story about work in my family is my father's decision, early in his career as a plumber, to choose to become a teacher of plumbing in a trade school rather than establish his own business. He knew well that he could make much more money in business, but he also knew that he loved to teach. He has always enjoyed teaching people anything, from plumbing to sports, and he has always had an intellectual curiosity about the natural world. In his teaching, he loved especially to study and talk about water and its place in society.

Over the years I think my mother and father regretted not having more money that could have come from a different decision, but they knew that my father had to go the route of the teacher. It was obvious to everyone in the family that he was born to teach. My father's greater concern about spiritual values he no doubt passed on to me.

Today many people are giving up their corporate positions for jobs that are more socially aware and in tune with their values. Some make the change dramatically, as if to prevent them from sliding back. Newspaper accounts tell of an executive in his tower office cleaving his desk with an ax. A concert pianist, frustrated with the emptiness he felt in his concert tours, shoved his piano out a second-story window.

Most people make the change less spectacularly. They may take a cut in pay to do work that aligns with their new vision and values. They may come to the realization that working for a company with corrupt values taints them and is ultimately immoral. Or maybe the work is just too pragmatic and doesn't speak to the need to do something worthwhile.

Ethics, a Part of Spiritual Practice

Spiritual practices like going to church, meditating, doing a spiritual kind of yoga, and praying have an effect on people's psychology and character. They grow to feel a strong sense of concern for humanity and want to do good in the world. They become more ethical through their spiritual sensitivities.

An older style of ethics teaches people simply to do the right thing, as a matter of principle. But today we can understand ethics as being more deeply rooted. You may be ethical because of your empathy for your neighbor, or because of your appreciation for the natural world and animals. You may understand how in society we are all interconnected, and that sense of world community inspires you to improve the level of ethical behavior around the world. Shaped by these deep ethical concerns, you may want to find work that embodies your values and doesn't create dissonance between your ethical ideas and the work you are doing.

If you work at a job that contradicts your ethics, you are divided, your personal values moving in one direction and your work in another. Since ethics has deep roots in your emotions and your vision, you will feel divided against yourself. Your work will be disturbing, and you will never get to the point where you feel you have found your life work. Ethics plays a deep and central role in this search.

You could be guided by your ethics toward the work you want. As you grow older, your ethical sensitivities will probably change and ripen. Your feeling of being more or less suited to the work you are doing will change accordingly. As your ethics develop, you can follow those changes and move toward the kind of work that satisfies you. Part of you that has to be fulfilled is your spirituality, and part of that spirituality is your sense of values.

The path toward a life work is a dynamic process. It goes through many phases, for most people. As you develop as a person, your ideas about work shift accordingly and move closer to your goal of a meaningful job. Be true to your ethics, and you have a better chance of knowing what to do in life.

Following through on your values brings you into a bigger world—a form of transcending—where you have to grow into a bigger person. Nelson Mandela became a lawyer and practiced with the poor. That experience led him to local leadership in the reform of apartheid society and finally to the presidency of his country. He was led by an ethical calling and became who he is by means of that call to improve the life of his people.

Business as a Spiritual Practice

If anything in our everyday lives appears to be purely secular, it is business. The focus on money, marketing, and profits seems to move in a direction exactly opposite that of spirituality. And yet, today business leaders attend conferences and workshops on spirituality with the fervent hope that it will help their businesses and their personal lives. Many feel soiled by working only for profit and in making money their primary value. They are looking for options.

It is not enough to link spirituality with business or add it on as an extra. You can discover spiritual elements within the practice of business itself and then make them more visible and effective.

When the spirituality inherent in business becomes clearer, workers might have a better chance of doing work that inspires them and helps them conceive of what they are doing as their life work.

The spirituality in work is fully and completely compatible with enjoying the work, attending to details, and hoping for a profit. I see the marketing of my books as part of my spiritual practice, and my hopes for financial success support the spirituality of my work. Money can become an obstacle, but in itself it is a key ingredient in a meaningful life.

Business, even with its concern for profit, has an important role in the community, providing goods and services, offering jobs and financial support for community activities. These are all ways to foster community and move beyond the focus on company profit. A business also creates a workplace, which can be merely pragmatic and efficient, or it could embody spiritual values like beauty, community, friendship, craft, generosity, and hospitality.

In a small town in New Hampshire near where I live now and where my children grew up, two men run a movie house that truly nurtures the soul of the community. They have one small hall and a second smaller room in the upper level of the old Town Hall. It is all "retro" in the extreme. They get films, both popular and artistic, that they consider of good quality, and they charge one-third the price you would pay in a small city. The seats are old but comfortable, and in the winter you are advised to wear a jacket. The theater attracts people from neighboring towns and is part of the life of the community.

What is "spiritual" about this theater? Probably its capacity to serve people at a very human scale with heart and imagination. Going there, you don't feel you're paying the stockholders of some megacorporation. You're being part of a real neighborhood community. The two men who run this business decided, like Nasrudin, not to follow the logic of Cineplex but rather to offer quality films and create a warm focus for the life of their community. Just being there, you are filled with the spirit of community, and I know that many people go to this theater for that spirit as well as for the movie.

The Spirituality of the Workplace

A major resource for the spiritual life is nature, and businesses could plan carefully so that the workplace has a positive connection with nature. Many businesses are situated near rivers and other bodies of water. Rather than just use these as physical resources for manufacturing, a business could tap into the spiritual quality of rivers and lakes, keeping them clean and making them accessible to workers.

Spiritual traditions also recommend building with the basic elements of life. If the company is not located near water, it could channel it into the workplace. I have visited hospitals and schools where water flows beneath the floors and you walk over bridges inside the building, enjoying the water. Stone and wood, iron and clay, also suggest the primal qualities of the earth and have a spiritual air.

The indoor waterfall—water cascading over stone—has become popular. That and other ways of making the workplace more elemental might create a more spiritual atmosphere. Ponds, basins of water, fireplaces, raw wood furnishings—these small things evoke the spirits of nature.

We also have centuries of great spiritual art from numerous traditions that can be brought to the workplace to charge the atmosphere spiritually. Business leaders often appreciate inspirational quotes; these could be substantial and come directly from long-standing spiritual traditions.

Spiritual masters often recommend silence as an effective route to spiritual awareness; yet workplaces are often noisy. It might help to have places of retreat, if not more serious attention to the quality of sound. It's difficult to be contemplative and mindful when your ears are being assaulted. A library of spiritual works might seem odd for a secular business, but such a thing could also be a valuable resource for workers.

Food always has spiritual connotations and possibilities. Satish Kumar, founder of Schumacher College in England, often tells how he created a community school in his small town by focusing the day's lessons and activities around making lunch. Making and eating food together can be a profound spiritual experience, especially when repeated day after day. Yet how many companies consider the quality of food and the manner in which it is eaten as an essential part of the workplace?

All of these suggestions relate to the life work of everyone involved with a particular company, from the CEO to the last-hired worker. It is difficult to find your life work when most of the jobs you try show little evidence of a spiritual dimension. A life work is a spiritual thing. It goes infinitely deep into your reason for living. If you are in search of a life work, you might explore companies in which the spirituality is not hidden and in fact shapes the work and its environment.

Contemplation

Living and working in line with our values and morals and making the world a better place is one way to bring spirituality to work. But there are quieter aspects of work that also serve a spiritual purpose.

Some jobs, especially those that are dull and repetitious, offer opportunities for contemplation. Meditation is a formal way of tuning out the external life and focusing inwardly. Contemplation is getting so absorbed that you lose awareness of where you are and what you are doing. The Zen master recommends being completely caught up in what you are doing at the moment. Seung Sahn told his students: "When you eat, eat." But one day they saw him eating and reading the newspaper. They asked him about it. He answered: "When you eat and read the newspaper, just eat and read the newspaper."

Certain kinds of work offer an opportunity to be absorbed and for a while lose a consciousness of self. Engaged in such work, you contemplate not abstractly but concretely. You are taken over by the work and the work becomes not just prayer, but contemplative prayer. You lose the sense that is almost always with you of being a person doing something. In contemplative acts, you are simply doing.

But there is a difference between being bored by a repetitive job and using it as a path to contemplation. You allow the mindlessness of the work to become no-mind. You enter more fully and intentionally into the repetition and enjoy the lack of consciousness. In that state of absorption, you allow inspirations to come into you, because contemplation doesn't have to be empty and pure. It can be full of images and thoughts and inspirations.

Contemplation is also a quieting of inner and outer activity. It produces calm and allows some relief from the frenetic activity of ordinary life and from the incessant thoughts connected to various anxieties. It can be brief and yet effective, and so even short periods of repetitious work can offer the opportunity for a quieting of the self that stands at the edge of spiritual contemplation.

The Jungian analyst Marie-Louise von Franz once observed that a person cutting vegetables while preparing to cook food is full of daydreams and fantasies that nurture the life of the soul. Contemplation can be an absorption in work that is free of self-consciousness and yet rich with imagination.

Serious meditators understand that life offers opportunities all day long for seizing the moment and withdrawing from busyness, if only for a short time. You can do this intentionally and turn ordinary moments into miniature meditations. You make them part of your spiritual life, making monotonous work almost like chanting—a monotone moment that can be either just plain dull or a time for reflection.

In my own life as a writer, it might be the time when I look on a shelf for a book or sit reading a manuscript or go upstairs or walk or take a shower and think. These are quiet, dull, yet fertile moments, and they occur in many people's work lives. It helps to know the traditions of contemplation and then see how ordinary life offers opportunities for reflection.

Christian monks have a saying that shifts the intention of their work to a different plane: *Laborare est orare*—"To work is to pray." Monks place a high value on work, though the work they do is often quite ordinary. They almost never work for money, but they see value for themselves and their community in cooking and cleaning, building and repairing, sewing and farming, and making bread and wine.

They seek out menial labor because it is humbling, but not in some masochistic, self-effacing sense. It gets them involved in the basic needs of their community, allowing them to offer service and get their hands dirty in the ordinary tasks of an ordinary life. In this they are not too different from Wallace Stevens wanting to go to work to be like everyone else.

Monks desire a lifestyle that wholly embodies their spiritual vision of equality, community, and service. They want to build this lifestyle from the ground up, on their own terms. And so they make their own bread and build their own barns, and take care of their own animals. Their labor is the manifestation of their ideals and their piety, and so it is truly a form of prayer.

The Jesuit visionary Teilhard de Chardin described the basic human task as carrying on the evolution of the natural world. Ecology, care of the environment, can be planetary in scope and yet begin at home. Monks around the world know this and so they spend precious time growing crops and cleaning toilets. The difference is that through their intention they turn their toil into a form of prayer. They are participating in the unfolding of humanity as they fix a squeaky door and milk the cows. They have a transcendent purpose that extends all the way down to the most ordinary daily chores.

This mixture of vision, intention, and care transforms the experience of work, giving any form of labor a spiritual dimension. Nasrudin doesn't get any worldly praise for not working with the same values as his coworkers; he has a different goal.

The more transcendent your vision, the more personal and profound your participation in your work and the satisfaction you take from it. If you approach your job unconsciously and just go through the motions, you will be like everyone else who does similar work. But if you press your ideas to the extreme, meditate on them, sort them through, and apply them at work, your efforts will be that much more individual because of your reflection. You will be more conscious as you take up your work, and your ideas and values will be so clarified that they will show in your labor.

I once visited the shop of a woodworker in Ireland. He had selected only woods grown on plantations, so as not to use endangered trees. He used nontoxic oils for polishing. He kept the organic colors and shapes of the wood in his finished bowls rather than cutting them away. In all these ways he presented a philosophy of life as much as a practical bowl, and his satisfaction at work seemed all the more solid for his ideas. Whenever I use his bowl in my home, his values come to mind and once more I am inspired. His ideas make the bowl special and unique. This is concrete work with a spiritual dimension.

Spirituality without a ground in daily work tends to be abstract and ultimately irrelevant. Practical labor without a spiritual base is unconscious, narcissistic, and one-dimensional. It lacks the richness of good ideas, deep ethics, and inspiration. The spiritual and the practical need each other. Without the spiritual, work is a mere job.

Mystery

A key element in the spiritual life is an appreciation for mystery. We live in a society that sees a mystery as a challenge, and you are successful only if you dispel the mystery and replace it with an explanation.

Religion takes a different approach to the mysterious. Rather than try to explain it away, it creates ritual and song and story around the mystery, holding it and revering it. Religion assumes that a mystery is valuable in itself. It is not a code waiting to be broken. It is a powerful, unfathomable truth that is to be honored and lived.

The mystery of love, the mystery of the universe, the mystery of marriage and children, the mysterious life of animals, the mysteries of birth and death—all of these give human life its infinite depth. Without them we end up with mere explanation, which may be satisfying at one level but is not humanizing.

A life work is one of those inexplicable mysteries that resists reasonable explanation. If we were to take the lead from religions, we would honor the mysteriousness of a calling. We would find it precious without any need to take it apart and figure it out. We wouldn't have to control it or demand anything of it.

A life work is nothing less than the mystery of who we are. It can't be equated with a job or a career. It isn't just an emotion, nor is it an illusion. It is of the greatest importance for feeling complete and tranquil. Yet it is impossible to define and control. It is profoundly spiritual and can only be approached with the sense that we are connected somehow to the world in which we live and to people who have passed on and have sought and perhaps discovered their life work.

Every day I walk past a cemetery in our small town and think about the lives of the people at rest there. The truth is, I talk to them as I go by. I see them as a little community. I think about their individual lives and the work they did. Somehow I think that cemetery holds the secret to what I am looking for: my life work, some meaning to my life, a purpose and an inspiration. I know that I am headed there shortly, and I hope that the simple things I have done with my life, which has been so full of mistakes and wrong turns, will add up to a real opus, a meaningful work, a life fully lived.

The alchemist peers into his retort. The mass of material has been stewing there for days, weeks, or even months. The heat has been constant, sometimes red-hot, sometimes just simmering. He imagines he sees a white bird, this time flying down into the material, time after time. This is the bird of spirit, an inseminating figure that represents vision, values, ethics, philosophy, compassion, and spiritual understanding. It brings the primal stuff to life, refines it, matures it, and ultimately completes the project.

The confusion eases into order, ignorance into understanding. Raw material now becomes more sophisticated. The mass of stuff takes on beautiful forms. Where the Work began in chaos, it now coalesces as a world takes shape. The alchemist looks closer and imagines he sees a human figure emerging from the ooze and mist in the vessel. The homunculus, the little person, appears, like Adam or Eve, a new man and a new woman. Alchemy has created a person.

CHAPTER TWELVE

A SEAMLESS LIFE

*I am convinced that to maintain one's self on this earth is not
a hardship but a pastime, if we will live simply and wisely. It is
not necessary that a man should earn his living by the sweat
of his brow, unless he sweats easier than I do.*

HENRY DAVID THOREAU

When the alchemical Work is almost at an end, the alchemist notices a variety of colors shimmering in the
stuff that has been cooking. He imagines that he sees
a peacock's tail there, a display of iridescent feathers and luminous
colors. He knows that the magical stone is not far away now and
soon the Work may be completed.

The image of the peacock is remarkable at this stage of the
Work. You might expect the many different things that have gone
into the opus now to become one. Instead, a multicolored bird is
presented as the penultimate goal—the stone or elixir comes last.
Some alchemists thought that the feathers stood for the planets of
astrology, which in turn represented the focal points of a life, from
Jupiter's sense of community to Venus's insistence on love and sex

to Mercury's skills at commerce and communication. Certainly the alchemists understood that the maturing of a life is a gathering of many things, each having its own worth and importance.

Connecting the image of the rainbow bird tail to our search for a life work, we might understand that our life task is always multi-faceted. It is not one thing. We may be inspired to move in a certain direction, but our activities will be multiple and varied and often contradictory.

So what is your life work? Your career, your service to the community, raising your family, maturing into a solid person, or all the things you do in your spare time? Or is your life work something more mysterious that rises out of all of these things? We might even ask at this late point, is there a life work after all? Or is the idea of a calling only a fantasy that eggs us on and allows us to accomplish things?

Passages

In the story of Mahud, this simple man moves willingly from one job to another without any apparent plan or direction. He is extraordinarily obedient to the call of the angel, and in the end he seems to find himself. And yet the person he becomes seems to have little relation to the work he did to prepare for it. Was it the many jobs that made him a healer and teacher or was it his sheer obedience?

His story is one of passages. We are all aware of the journey aspect of a life work, how you go from one job to another, not always on an upward track but moving along nonetheless. But the life passages from childhood to adolescence to adulthood to retirement are not only stages in a life; they are initiations of the heart and soul.

When you go from one phase to another, you don't just move; you change as a person. You go through qualitative transformations that leave you, in the end, far different from who you were at the beginning.

These initiations don't always coincide with the obvious phases of life. You may get married, for instance, and not truly shift your identity from the life of a single person to that of a couple. There is no guarantee that the ceremony or intention to shift will make it happen. Yet, if you are not initiated into married life, you will probably find marriage difficult, if not impossible. The same is true at work. If you are given increased responsibilities but don't advance personally as a leader, you may not succeed. External behavior follows a shift in character.

You might also go through more phases than people think are standard. Many men and women wake up one morning in their married life to discover that they have changed in some way. Suddenly they may crave more meaningful work and activities. They now have to adjust to a different status, and their partner also has to deal with the change. You may wake up changed in relation to work. You may no longer be satisfied with the work you are doing and fantasize about a more exciting future.

Initiations take place many times in the course of a life, and if they don't happen, the person may feel stuck in an inappropriate place in life. Some people never grow into married life but always think of themselves as single, even though outwardly they are married. Some people create a business but never feel equipped to lead. You can see profound difficulties at work arising from these conflicts between personal development and the structures of a career.

A life work is made up of many life-altering initiations, and the most successful people, in the deeper sense of the word, will have changed from one phase to another. One initiation, perhaps achieved with considerable struggle, will lead to another.

Passages are more subtle than we often imagine them to be. For example, a person who reaches the age of retirement may now be ready for the job of his life. He now knows himself or has finally developed highly sophisticated skills, and he is ready to work.

Many people resist retirement because they want to keep working. There is nothing wrong in this resistance; it may indicate only that the person is now ready for another kind or level of work activity. On the other hand, some people enter retirement and are not prepared for it. They become lost and depressed because they haven't gone through the necessary initiation or change in attitude.

In my work I have met many limo drivers. They usually love their work, and for many the driver's job is one they picked up after retiring from a career in business. Several have told me how much they enjoy the absence of stress as drivers. They have irregular hours and have to get up very early sometimes, but the scope of their job is limited, and that is significant to them after a challenging life in business. Most of them say that although their career was in management or sales, driving certainly qualifies as a portion of their life work.

A life work is like a peacock's tail: It has many facets. As you go from one job to another, you begin to see who you are and what you might do with your life. All the jobs may contribute to that realization and therefore play a significant role. Even the dead-end jobs, the ones you suffered through, the ones that seemed to go nowhere—all of them may be redeemed at some future point when it is revealed to you what you are meant to do.

These developments may sound dramatic, but in real life they may be quite simple. Most of us are not called to fame and fortune.

Our ordinary jobs may look simple on the outside, but we may feel them intensely. Our life work is largely about our *experience* of life on the planet and not necessarily any external measure of our accomplishment.

A Work of Life

When we say we have a calling or want to do the work we are meant to do, we are raising big issues about the whole of life. Your career may be going well in one direction, while the activity that really gives you a sense of accomplishment is something else entirely.

A life work is the work of your life, meaning that your whole life is a work, and every aspect of it can make a contribution to your sense of calling. You may be absorbed in your career, but you can't ignore the importance of being a parent as part of your calling in life. Knowing that the career is only a piece of the whole, you might give it considerable attention and energy but not your whole devotion. You may work out tensions between your job and your family from the conviction that both are important aspects of your work life.

Some people feel burned out by their jobs. They give so much of themselves to the job that they have nothing to give elsewhere, or they reach a point where they feel they have nothing else to give anywhere. Burnout can arise from many different conditions, one being an excessive focus on only one aspect of your life work. This exclusive focus tends to be on the job rather than other important areas of life.

Just as the feathers of the peacock's tail belong to the one peacock, so the various facets of your work are part of your life. They are many and yet they coalesce into a self, into an individual person doing many things. They are connected to one another and dependent on one another.

I have a friend, Emily, who has a Ph.D. in literature. She has spent her life so far raising her children, singing in church choirs, developing a small craft business, and writing. These four, plus her marriage and service to her community, are her *cauda pavonis*, her peacock's tail, the four parts of her calling.

In her art, she wishes that one form would "call" her, so she could devote herself to it. On the other hand, she sees that beneath all her artistic activities lies an unnamable "art" around which the others dance. That image sustains her as she feels pulled in several directions.

Emily is a highly intelligent, gifted, and complicated person who feels she hasn't yet made her full contribution to life. She comes from a family where men, not women, pursued their dreams, and she feels a strong obligation to help her extended family, or anyone else for that matter, whenever she senses their need. Sometimes that need to help gets in the way of her other work.

The multiple callings she has toward writing, craft, music, and family sometimes make her feel fragmented. On the other hand, she has accomplished a great deal in all these areas. Although she has yet to bring all her passions to a satisfying point of focus, she demonstrates both the richness of multifaceted vocation and the tensions such a calling entails.

Her friends are watching Emily to see if her writing will one day explode into a full-fledged, dominant career. For now, they admire the way she so intelligently and effectively attends to the peacock.

Overlapping "Jobs"

Although we work hard being students, parents, and citizens, we don't usually think of these activities as work in the same sense we consider our jobs work. Therefore we separate our lives into categories that do not impinge on one another. We become fragmented simply because of the way we imagine and label our activities. We put the entire onus of calling and meaning on our jobs, whereas other areas of life could carry some of that weight.

If you were to imagine parenthood, say, as a calling rather than a set of tasks, you might more easily see how you are fulfilled in raising children. You might take on the persona of parent with more authority and conviction and be less overwhelmed by its demands. Attitude is important in these matters, and attitude depends largely on imagination.

Today you often run into people who are "overworked," especially if they are trying to raise a family and hold down a job. Does "overworked" mean doing too many tasks, or does it refer to the lack of a philosophy that would give status and meaning to parenting? Our emotions are often affected by the way we imagine our situation. If you picture parenthood as a set of demands, you will suffer from it. If you picture it as a noble calling and a source of meaning, you might feel the burden less. You have a big, weighty image of who you are in this work, and that big image bears the burden of the labor involved.

Broadening the activities that you call work can also allow them to overlap. I sometimes bring my children with me on lecturing trips. This practice does not make travel easier, but it makes the experience of work richer and easier to bear. It is easier because then I am my full self before the public, and not some disembodied individual artificially separated from my role as a family man. And I have the support of my family life with me. I don't choose this approach for every trip, because I also like being an individual at times. But just the occasional family experience keeps my life together.

Your life work is about your life first. You can fail and quit and change and go down the ladder of success and still have a life work. You don't even have to understand how failure and instability have made you who you are. These things are often inscrutable. You only have to trust that your story is unfolding and you will eventually understand what it means.

A Many-Sided Life

Once you understand the breadth and depth of a life work, you may see how many "side" activities are part of the opus of your life. Travel, for instance, even as part of a vacation, can be an important part of the work of deepening your life. I once spoke with a friend in Ireland about her nineteen-year-old daughter going off on a journey around the world. The mother pictured this travel as an important step in her daughter's education. She believed that her daughter would benefit from seeing many cultures of the world before going on with her university learning. She saw her daughter's travel as an essential element in her maturation and the beginning of her work life. Travel can have such an impact on a person's worldview that it may also serve as a powerful initiation, a perfect activity for a young person entering adulthood.

Avocations in the arts, crafts, gardening, and collecting all have a deeper purpose that is not immediately visible, and that deeper purpose can make a hobby a more important work than a career or job. People who garden on weekends say that they enjoy feeling the clean earth on their fingers. Now, this is a strong experience of the psyche, not just the body. What is it about us that we need to have soil on our hands? Is it grounding, purity, a connection with nature, renewal, a cleansing of the soul?

My father has collected stamps for almost eighty-five years. He has spent countless hours taking used stamps off letters and parcels, preparing them for the albums, cataloging them and pricing them. He has become a stamp expert, but his career was in plumbing, a field he truly loved. I don't know the deep motive that led him to this hobby, but I do know that it put him in touch with a bigger world than he would have had as a plumber. He is in correspondence with collectors all over the world, and the stamps have educated him about cultures around the globe.

Avocations can be part of your life work, and you don't have to make them bigger than they are for them to belong there. The small things we do, the insignificant activities, can have a place in life much larger than they would seem to have. All human actions have a literal and a symbolic meaning, and gardening, collecting, and making crafts may be important as symbols as well as for what they achieve at the literal level.

Those who build and fly model airplanes probably have some of the flying boy spirit in them, the hot-air balloon desire to be disencumbered of too much reality. Maybe birders, too, have some of that spirit; otherwise, they might be studying fish or lions. Often it isn't easy to see the symbolic import of a hobby, but the devotion people bring to birding and collecting indicates that there is more going on deep in the experience than what appears on the surface.

The author of *Lolita*, Vladimir Nabokov, has puzzled his readers with his extraordinary talent for words blended with his passion for the study of butterflies. Many have attempted to understand the connection, but the symbolic thrust of an avocation is difficult to discern. You can make some connections, but you would have to do a thorough psychoanalysis to arrive at a convincing explanation. Nabokov himself said, "Frankly, I never thought of letters as a career. Writing has always been for me a blend of dejection and high spirits, a torture and a pastime—but I never expected it to be a source of income. On the other hand, I have often dreamt of a long and exciting career as an obscure curator of lepidoptera in a great museum."[1] From the writer's point of view, his study of butterflies came first in his life work, though he made his living in literature.

The Heart of Your Work Life

Maybe a life work is not a particular job, an occupation, a career, or a special role. Maybe it is a sense of oneself that emerges from a lifetime of moving, like Mahud, from one task to another, maybe even from one career to another. In some ways it is elusive, because it may require a certain mass of experience before it is revealed.

The final piece might come quite late, as it did for Christopher Reeve, whose life seemed clearly anchored in an acting career until he had a horseback riding accident and then became an advocate for quadriplegics. It is difficult to imagine President Jimmy Carter's life work without the contributions he made after he left the presidency. A life work may take an entire lifetime to show itself.

Therefore, you must remain open to the possibilities and resist the temptation to make a closure before your life has run out. This means always keeping your very identity open-ended, because a life work defines you. Spiritual writers sometimes say that all finite loves point to an infinite love, and so there is always a yearning for more. The same could be true of a life work. Any finite task or career points to another beyond it. Your sense of what you are meant to do with your life has to remain open-ended, no matter how much or how little you feel you have accomplished. You never know fully what you are called to do.

Toward the end of their work lives, many people feel that it's time to pass on their wisdom. They reach out to young people to teach them and support them. This is a noble and fulfilling sentiment, fully appropriate for the apparent end of a career. Perhaps your philosophy of a work life could include your own imagination of how your later years should be spent.

You may picture the arc of your life as beginning with a necessary focus on yourself and then opening to the world and finally giving to the young or giving back to a society that has supported you. This important gesture of gratitude is not just altruistic; it serves you by completing the dynamic of your heart whereby you struggle and labor, learn and receive, and then return your wisdom and experience as an elder.

Conclusion: The Opus of the Soul

Finding your life work is inseparable from maturing as a person and finding your place in society. To mature as a person you have to take considerable time sorting through, taking to heart, and resolving the mistakes and failures that have marked your progress. You have to refine the raw material of your emotions and jagged relationships, learning better how to engage the world effectively. You have to unleash your creativity in realistic ways, grounding your idealism and ambitions in real-world contexts.

You need a spiritual vision, a philosophy of life, and a deep and evolving sense of values. You need close relationships, participation in community, and openness to social need. With these personal qualities in place, you will glimpse the nature of your life work step-by-step and after a long while get a sense of its arc. Then you can help others find their way.

You can fashion a rich, multifaceted life that doesn't feel fragmented or broken. You can be led on by an inner daimon and by the demands of the world around you. Sometimes just responding to a local need gives you all the work you can handle and an identity as well. Because of your openness to the many calls you have heard and felt, whatever your career may have been, you can become a healer for others. You have gone down into the rich humus of human existence with your openhearted choices and your bittersweet struggles, and out of that initiation you can say the words and embody the vision that will heal others. In healing others, you will have found yet another calling and further complications and deeper rewards. Life is rich, and you will taste that richness when you stay close to the dynamic that is your life work.

ACKNOWLEDGMENTS

A few years ago Spencer Niles invited me to give a talk for career counselors in San Francisco. Rather than discuss jobs and the pursuit of a career, I decided to speak about the alchemical opus, the deep work of making a personality and a life. Sande Johnson, who was associated with an educational publisher, suggested then that I write a book on the theme. I'm grateful to both of them for their understanding of my peculiar way of seeing things.

In the writing of the book I had occasion to reflect on my own influences, starting with my father, Ben Moore, who at this writing is ninety-four years old and still busy with his life work of teaching, playing music, and helping people in general. He still has a job that he drives to four days a week.

I also think of my friends who are, like all of us, struggling to discover what that deep life work will be. Emily Archer, Pat Toomay, Steven Haley, Redmond O'Hanlon, Satish Kumar, Brendan and Hazel Hester, and our new neighbors—Tom, Dale, Jane, and Sally—have all helped me write this book. I'm grateful, too, to Brian Moss and other correspondents who have told me their stories.

Oddly, my work life had been running quite smoothly for fifteen years and suddenly got wobbly during the writing of this book. I have had to reimagine my life work, and as the book goes to the public I am reinventing myself yet another time. I'll have to reread these pages and get some ideas for myself. In this process I have had precious professional advice from Michael Katz, Bill Shinker, Hugh Van Dusen, Russell Donda, and Kristin Frykman. Amy Hertz and Kris Puopolo together helped me shape the book for a wide range of readers and taught me further lessons in the craft of writing.

I am grateful, too, to the people whose lives I mention as examples of the quest for a life work. Most of their stories are accurate, as I know them, and a few are adjusted for reasons of confidentiality. As always, Joan Hanley, shaping her life work in a remarkable way, inspires and instructs me as she follows a deep guidance in her. It also just happened that I began homeschooling my bright and sweet teenage daughter, Siobhán, while writing this book, and I have learned many new lessons about teaching and about the important work of being a father. My son, Abraham, started college during this period, and his extraordinary maturation into a fine young man has taught me a little about what it means to grow up in this complicated era. I always feel supported by my mother, who died four years ago.

This book is an opus, and like all creative work, it can only be accomplished by a community. I thank everyone who guided me in this work, including those I've neglected to name. The reader now will complete the work by reflecting on the ideas and adding to the making of our society.

CHAPTER TEN

1. *The Symbolic Life*, trans. R. F. C. Hull. *Collected Works*, vol. 18, paras 673.

NOTES

CHAPTER TWO

1. Quoted in Joan Richardson, *Wallace Stevens: The Later Years* (New York: William Morrow, 1988), p. 20.

2. Ibid., p. 72.

CHAPTER THREE

1. C. G. Jung, *The Symbolic Life*, trans. R. F. C. Hull, *Collected Works* (Princeton N.J.: Princeton University Press, 1976), vol. 18, §442.

CHAPTER FOUR

1. http://www.achievement.org/autodoc/page/mar0int-1.

2. http://www.achievement.org/autodoc/page/cas0int-1.

CHAPTER FIVE

1. Alexander Roob, *Alchemy and Mysticism* (Köln: Taschen, 1997), p. 175.

CHAPTER SIX

1. "Sweet Revenge," *BusinessWeek* (January 22, 2007).

CHAPTER NINE

1. Agnes de Mille, *Martha: The Life and Work of Martha Graham* (New York: Random House, 1991), p. 84

2. C. G. Jung, *Memories, Dreams, Reflections,* ed. Aniela Jaffé, trans. Richard and Clara Winston (New York: Pantheon Books, rev. ed. 1973), pp. 156–57.

3. Federico García Lorca, *In Search of Duende* (New York: New Directions, 1998), p. 51.

4. Ibid., p. 50.

CHAPTER TEN

1. C. G. Jung, "Psychology of the Transference," in *The Practice of Psychotherapy,* trans. R. F. C. Hull, *Collected Works* (Princeton, N.J.: Princeton University Press, 1966), vol. 16, p. 490.

CHAPTER ELEVEN

1. Shunryu Suzuki, *Zen Mind, Beginner's Mind* (New York and Tokyo: Weatherhill, 1970), p. 63.

CHAPTER TWELVE

1. See Brian Boyd, ed., "Nabokov, Literature, Lepidoptera," in *Nabokov's Butterflies* (Boston: Beacon Press, 2000), pp. 1–30.